CW01475178

ALL CHANGE

Clive Bradley

ALL CHANGE

Clive Bradley

A life in politics,
newspapers and books
to the start of
world-changing digital

Marble Hill

ALL CHANGE

First published by Marble Hill Publishers in 2024
Flat 58 Macready House
75 Crawford Street
London W1H 5LP
www.marblehillpublishers.co.uk

A CIP catalogue record for this book is available from the British Library.

ISBN: 9781738497058
E-ISBN: 9781738497065

Printed and bound by IngramSpark
Cover design by Paul Harpin
Typeset in Adobe Jenson and LDN Southbank

TABLE OF CONTENTS

The author's portrait was painted by Nuala Rowland.

ABOUT

I'VE A NUMBER of reasons for writing this book. I've had an enjoyable and interesting career in which I've got to know some famous people, mostly good, including Harold Wilson and his colleagues Denis Healey and Tony Benn of the Labour Party and the Labour Governments of 1964 and 1974; television pioneers like Grace Wyndham Goldie; great men of newspapers when they were still a major force in the land – Cecil King, Hugh Cudlipp, Rupert Murdoch, David Astor and, not so good, Robert Maxwell; less well known but no less a social and cultural force book publishers like Tom Maschler, Paul Hamlyn and George Weidenfeld. All this at a time when our way of life was being transformed, when the Print Revolution of the fifteenth century, which still governed how we shared information and ideas, was overturned by the Digital Revolution, when the ways of politics, broadcasting, newspapers, entertainment – indeed, the whole way in which we run our society – were radically changing.

When I was at the *Daily Mirror* in the late Sixties and early Seventies, it had a daily circulation of around five and a half million. As I write in 2024, coming on the age of 90 – an age which not long ago was thought largely unattainable – the *Daily Mirror*'s sale of printed copies is just quarter of a million. But the Red Top claims that its websites now have some 32 million readers a month online.

In this book, I tell something of my career, the people I met, and my increasing relationship with the digital revolution. Without any planning, I gravitated to becoming a manager, or problem solver, of difficult projects, usually under intense time pressure. After schools, national service and universities, I started at the BBC, moved to the Labour Party as broadcasting aide to Harold Wilson just a year before the 1964 general election, became a political journalist and national newspaper executive, appointed by the *Observer* to set up its own production plant and buildings a year before the end of its contract with the *Times*. I represented book publishing as Margaret Thatcher imposed her free market ideas and digital emerged as a new threat. And then the highlight of bringing together the main content industries' associations in an effective group to lobby, and work with, government with a strength justified by their importance to Britain's economy, society and global influence.

Like most revolutions, few of us had any idea how it would turn out. And, as with all revolutions, it wasn't long before the initial optimism began to wear off. As the realisation of new, possibly golden, opportunities dawned, new dot.com opportunities were grasped by ambitious entrepreneurs offering all sorts of services (primarily social media) to the public. Some were highly successful, most failed or were absorbed by the successful. New global tech giants – the likes of Microsoft, Google, Amazon, Facebook, Apple and Twitter, alongside a new type of company, Information Service Providers offering broadband communication – soon dominated the market, testing governments' regulatory powers.

Back in the Nineties and Noughties, we started to recognise that criminals, hackers, political extremists, dictators and other disrupters would exploit new information services, invade secret databases, spread *dis*information, fake news and conspiracy theories. In the Twenty Twenties, this has become a global priority, part of the conflict between East and West. Launching new technology was the easy part. Ensuring that the technology would deliver fast, reliable services that brought new prosperity to the world, with fair rewards for providers and consumers, proved more difficult. As I write, we worry about Artificial Intelligence which, like its many forerunners, offers enormous benefits – and a serious risk of running amok.

I had a good start. My father, Alfred Bradley, was director of administration at the Ford Motor Company in Dagenham in the Fifties. Long before computers became essential and ubiquitous, he foresaw how they could help resolve the management problems facing a car manufacturer such as Ford: cascades of data on payroll, finance, human resources, and the vast and complex spare parts stock. The days of Powers Samas punched cards as the way of sorting data were coming to an end. Lyons, the tea shop group, faced similar problems and my father invested Ford's money to develop, with them, the first computer for commercial business use, LEO (the Lyons Electronic Office).

When I joined the International Publishing Corporation (IPC) as political editor of the *Statist* magazine in 1965, one of my first interviews was with computer guru Stafford Beer, the group's technical development director. Beer planned to use computing and remote networking, both little understood at the time, to revolutionise the production of national newspapers. Ted 'Pick' Pickering, IPC Newspapers' editorial director, asked me to write a feature for the *Statist* on Beer's projects. This was republished, at length, in the *UK Press Gazette* (although few readers, I suspect, took the technology seriously). Years later, when I attended conferences about this new world, I was quietly proud when experts came up to ask if I was related to Alfred Bradley.

My mother, Kathleen Bradley, was a journalist, an early

woman reporter on the *Daily News* (later the *News Chronicle*) in Fleet Street in the Twenties. I owe them both eternal gratitude for their massive contributions to my life.

My apologies for the no doubt many errors and omissions, particularly failing to thank so many valued colleagues and friends who contributed so much but who get taken for granted. Apologies too for glossing over many disasters, mistakes and bad decisions. We made errors and we know it. I hope I am reasonably truthful about them here. And my particular thanks to Paul Simpson for his expert and thoughtful help in preparing this book.

Finally apologies to all those with whom I have disagreed and to whom I may have been (just a little) less than respectful.

ACT 1
START UP

Chapter 1:

Upminster Boy

UPMINSTER IS A not very important town in the not very important London borough of Havering in south Essex, east of London, but it is where I grew up and I was happy there. Not many celebrities come from Upminster – William Joyce, 'Lord Haw-Haw', Second World War traitor, was a rare if unfortunate exception. The talented punk singer and polio victim Ian Dury grew up in Upminster and loved it. He dedicated an album, Lord Upminster, and a lyric, *Upminster Boy*, to the town. He died there, too young, in 2000. Nowadays there's also an electronic music festival, We Are FSTVL, on the local airfield. It's said to be the world's best.

I am not very much a real Upminster boy, but I too enjoyed the town, with its ancient parish church (very high church: for a short time I would go there, after being confirmed, as a blue-eyed fair-haired boy, dressed in an alb with purple collar, and swing the censer with the best of them), stately Congregational Church, which we attended regularly when I was young (very intelligent – one minister told me I was a Zoroastrian – but in spite of him I am now a convinced atheist), beautiful smock windmill (a photo I took graced the cover of *The Lady* magazine), the Abrahams – old milling family and local bakers, Roome's Stores, the Cosy Corner café with the Delft-tiled United Dairies and jellied veal, the old Bell pub, parks, spacious Upminster Common, nearby gorgeous Childerditch, the Queen's Theatre in Hornchurch and Saturday morning Odeon, excursions to Southend (which we snobbily called Westcliff). We didn't lack for things to keep us happy in the school holidays.

The town is probably best known for being located at the east end of the District Line and for being hailed, with some hype, as the first garden suburb back in the Thirties, the result of town planning, the arrival of the District Line in 1934, a new arterial road passing it on the north between east London and Southend, and the relocation of Ford's giant car factory (everything from blast furnace to polished car) from Trafford Park, Manchester, to nearby Dagenham. Part of a circle of towns outside east London which are conspicuously middle-middle-class – neither part of the East End nor home to the stereotypical 'Essex Man'. Upminster remains a good place to live, within easy reach of the City and Ford. It was notable, for a time, as a place where teenagers threw wild parties when their parents were away.

The town's proximity to Ford during the war changed my future. Being east of Dagenham and on the District Line, it was on the flight path for German bombers on their missions to blitz 'the works' and the East End. With the town so close to the front line of the air war, parents were desperate to evacuate their children. Some Ford offspring were dispatched, unhappily, to Canada. Pauline and I were evacuated to boarding schools in England.

Thankfully, Upminster suffered relatively little damage compared with London and other big cities. Towards the end of the war, it was on the flight path for doodlebugs (V1s) and rockets (V2s). You could hear doodlebugs coming, but the rockets were silent. One destroyed some houses only a few hundred yards from us, killing the occupants. When we went to look, there was just a vast hole. This was Hitler's last, failed gamble.

After a single hellish term (or was it a hellish two?) in 1940 at a convent school relocated from Upminster to Chilton in the Aylesbury Vale, which reluctantly accepted us Protestants, my eight-year-old sister Pauline and my five-year-old self (both raised as Congregationalists) rebelled. Pauline went to Milton Mount College, temporarily based in Lynton in Devon, while I was to go to Felsted Prep School, evacuated to a country mansion at Canon Frome near Ledbury in Herefordshire.

The original Canon Frome mansion, owned by General Ralph Hopton, one of Charles I's generals during the Civil War, had been besieged by Oliver Cromwell, who also slept there (Daphne du Maurier's masterpiece, *The King's General*, tells the story of a Civil War siege). As late as 1936 Canon Frome had a butler, footmen, cooks and maidservants before we small boys took over.

We returned in peacetime, Pauline to Milton Mount College back in Crawley in Sussex and I back to Felsted School in Essex (where Oliver Cromwell's son Richard had been educated before briefly ineffectually inheriting the Lord Protectorship). We both continued as fee-paying boarders, avoiding yet another change. But I strongly oppose children, even teenagers, being sent to boarding school. Quite apart from the separation from family, you spend all your time with children from the same middle class background and lose touch with the social diversity of your home town.

Felsted was still austere, a rather barrack-like existence, and not designed for boys like me who were bad at, and uninterested in, sport. As I write, the newspapers are full of articles by public school boys who were sent to sadistic prep schools, allegedly to prepare them for lonely service ruling the Empire, a promise not to be fulfilled. Well, thankfully Felsted wasn't half as bad as them. My main feeling was that I just had to endure. You got a decent education and a few of us were prepared for university. Discipline was strict, but, well, undisciplined, with school prefects carrying out beatings with the ready agreement of the housemaster – something regarded with horror today. I usually managed to avoid it, and when it happened, I suspect it was mainly because it was thought to be about time that Bradley was taught a lesson.

I never rose above the lowly status of house prefect, and that for only one term, the term I was preparing for university entrance and scholarships, so had little time to worry about boys' minor misdemeanours. Apart from some educational success, I did have one achievement, which was to become Company Sergeant Major, the topmost rank, in the school cadet force, which gave me two hours of illusory power, mindful that the head of school, only a corporal, would be head of school again as soon as we got out of our uniforms.

That rank led to what could have been a disaster for me (like Prince Edward). The 'regular' sergeant major, a genial former Royal Marine, 'Arge' Hart, told me that the school had been visited by the Royal Marine's recruitment team, and he had put me forward for service as a commando. This was not a role I saw myself in. Luck – or perhaps God - was on my side.

The next holiday I was cycling past RAF Hornchurch in south Essex, and stopped to read the noticeboard outside the guard-room. In two weeks' time there was to be a selection course for aircrew – apply within. I was told there was a vacancy. The course involved the usual officer selection challenges – two three foot planks to get across a four foot ditch. I would have been selected but proved to be colour blind, unacceptable for aircrew. However, if I joined the RAF for National Service a few months away, I had now been selected for a commission. I was able to go back to school for my last term and announce that I was to be commissioned in the RAF (exact role unspecified).

Felsted, ten years of my childhood – and thirty years of my adult life - deserves longer treatment. As I got more senior, life improved, you had friends, a study, and some teachers who were first class. So you have some happy memories. I was, for example, the boy who discovered the fire that ravaged the Grignon Hall. When you were in the sixth form, you could stay moderately late in the Bury, one of the school's better attributes, the home for the extra-curricular societies. I was walking back to my boarding house when I saw a strange glow in the hall in front of me. I ran grabbing a fire extinguisher and pressed the fire alarm, summoning the fire brigade and, more slowly, a host of boys and staff. My old enemy, now head of my house, an exact contemporary since the age of eight or so, saw me and ordered me back to bed. I took no notice.

In the early Seventies, I was selected by the Essex MPs as a governor of Felsted, and sat on the board for thirty years, the last few as chair of the academic committee. During this time, the school changed existentially for the better. It became co-educational. Food was enormously improved by the building of a new dining hall, with self-service and a wider menu. A music school was built, a new arts centre set up in the old laundry, where mess is no problem. There's a sports hall and hard pitches for winter sports, more diversity in sports to widen their appeal. I campaigned successfully for the International Baccalaureate as a wider, more challenging alternative to A-levels, and for of a separate 'house' for the growing number of day pupils to improve their status within the system. We set up a separate boarding unit for upper six pupils, to give them at age 17-18 a more collegiate life. The teaching staff expanded and more subjects were taught. We appointed an extraordinarily gifted woman as head of the prep school. and she transformed it into a world leader. The atmosphere of the whole school became more inviting, more pleasant for everyone, from new pupils up. It is now a different, and first class, school.

The problem is that facilities such as these cannot be afforded in most schools in the state system. Governments have tried to compensate by reducing some of the built-in advantages: it's not so easy now for public school pupils to get into Oxbridge, reducing one incentive for parents to pay the enormous fees. But in spite of policies such as removing the charity status of public (i.e. private) schools, so that parents become liable to VAT, possibly at a reduced rate, there is no way that they can be abolished – the government cannot afford to take something like a million more pupils into the state system, already dramatically over-stretched.

Back to the war and basic survival, my parents had to find ways in which we could live and sleep safely at home. We had a variety of shelters for the nights: an Anderson shelter dug into the lawn, which we never used as it promptly flooded from garden drains broken by the excavation; a cripplingly damp and mouldy double-brick outhouse, and a series of girders and sandbags in the kitchen which dribbled sand into our dried egg omelettes at supper time. Ultimately, we had a Morrison (named after Herbert Morrison, the Labour Home Secretary in the wartime government), a steel-plated table which slept eight, including five neighbours (my father didn't join us, as he had to go out as a fire watcher during air raids, kitted out with tin hat, bucket of water and sand scoop). The Morrison table came in handy for my Trix electric train, but I liked to sleep in the cupboard under the stairs with my sleeping bag, boy scout knife and teddy bear, where, I was assured, I would be safe even if the house collapsed around us.

My mother and father were both considerable achievers. My father moved with Ford from Manchester to Dagenham and became Director of Administration, later becoming president of the Office Management Association. My mother was an early woman reporter on the *Daily News* in Fleet Street in the early Twenties. Born Annie Kathleen Turner, she preferred her middle name Kathleen. They married when she was already 32, latish, probably by choice but also because at the time, soon after the First World War, young men were tragically in short supply. And when she married, she had to give up work to fulfil her duties as a wife. I write about them both later.

More, briefly, about family and partners. My sister, Pauline, my older sister, the wrong way round – it's much easier if the boy comes first – was a good looking and feisty woman who was never able to fulfil her potential. Like many women of her generation, she never had the opportunity to go to university, which she regretted all her life.

She married, young, to David Hunt, who led a tank squadron across Normandy to Hamburg during the invasion of France in 1944 and became a Major at the age of 22. Planning to be a school teacher, David was every bit a public school headmaster in the making. They met on one of our family holidays in Broadstairs, Pauline carried away, literally, on his motorbike, on which he also came down to take her out from school, to the intense jealousy of her friends. As I say, she was feisty. Over dinner, once, she was discussing the dreadful behaviour of the senior girls with the newbies. "Come to think of it", she suddenly added, "I was probably the worst of the lot!" For a younger brother, how true – but character will out.

For family reasons – his mother and father, devout Plymouth Brethren (or nearly), wanted to get away from London before the nuclear apocalypse they anticipated and bought a farm on the safer Somerset/Devon borders – David became a dairy farmer instead. And so, just south of Exmoor, Pauline and David raised a family of three boys: Timothy, the eldest, became a software architect in the United States (he was hired by Goldman Sachs to defeat the Millennium Bug, and would stay in a suite at the Savoy when in London); Jonathan, a journalist and leader of the Liberal Democrats in Birmingham, the largest local authority in the United Kingdom, and Paul, a graphic artist who settled in Liverpool. Jonathan and his wife Marcia, whose family came from Jamaica, have three children, also all boys, Andrew, Peter and Thomas. Together, Pauline and David made a major contribution to life in Dulverton and East Anstey. In 1961, I was asked to bid for them in the auction of a small farm a few miles from the main farm, Higher Sowerhill. Facing strong opposition, I upped our final bid from £5000 to £5050, and they became the loving owners of Cruwys Ball, which was then in a state of feudal dereliction. Done up, it became a marvellous home with fine views of the Devon countryside.

For myself, the Australian Lloyd Carleton was my partner from 1965 until he died of Aids in 1994, and then the Scottish John Lockhart, our friend from the mid-Seventies, became my civil partner under the new regime for same-sex couples. We lived together in Richmond until he died in 2018. The quartet was completed by Eric Beer (English), a close friend who usefully ran restaurants, loved to organise dinner parties – and drinks parties – for us, accompanied me on numerous overseas travels and often stayed at the apartment which John and I bought in Santa Eulalia in northern Ibiza. Sadly, I lost his companionship too when he died ten years ago. I must also appreciate two great friends, Geoff Davis, who has done building works and much more for me for some thirty years - I call him my factotum - and Rita Cobbina, equally long serving, who looked after my house – and me - in Richmond for an equally long time, including moving in for support during the long pandemic lock-downs.

I did National Service before university, which was encouraged because it was thought to make you more mature as an undergraduate. As a pilot officer in the RAF, I was disappointed not to be sent abroad, but enjoyed my job at a training base mainly for motor mechanics and fitters, with parachute packing and a few other essential skills added in. I was adjutant of one of the training wings, responsible for the Orderly Room and basic administration of about a thousand airmen and airwomen. The trainees appreciated the chance to be taught a useful skill, and caused little trouble. Some had been released from borstal or reform school on condition they signed on for four years.

I had two fatherly wing commanders, Cole and Davies, both of whom had served in the engineering training school at

Halton before the war. Recruit training at the top of icy Cannock Chase at RAF Hednesford was less fun, but probably no worse than boarding school. Admin training at Bircham Newton in north Norfolk was more like college. Officer training first at Millom in Cumberland and then at Jurby on the Isle of Man was tougher, but we spent a lot of the remainder of our course learning slow marching for the funerals of our group captain, wing commander and squadron leader who had tragically crashed into Snaefell on a preparatory visit to our new base.

Finishing second on the course, I was adjutant on the passing out parade, even though, on one exercise, the RAF Regiment Sqadron Leader Mad Mike suddenly put me in command. I placed my troops skilfully down the road only to hear the enemy trucks coming up from the rear. If I'd had a map, I might have realised that the Isle of Man is a small island with a road around its coast.

I am proud of the time when I was able to help save one of our trainees from impending misfortune. Lawrence, was, like his namesake T E Lawrence, returning from a weekend pass on his motorbike when he crashed into a tree. As adjutant, it was my duty to visit him in hospital in Wigan to hold a 'court of inquiry' into the circumstances of the accident. I found him wrapped in bandages from head to foot and he told me, as best he could, how urgently he wanted to see me. He had a problem. He was due to be married a week later. Obviously I replied that he would have to postpone. "No, sir, it's not like that."

As I knew the diocesan – very senior – bishop, a friend of my mother in their youth, I took the chance of phoning him to ask if he could arrange for Lawrence to be married in the hospital chapel. "Not if you're telling me that he jumped the gun," the bishop replied. Disheartened, I phoned the Wigan registrar. "No problem", he told me. He'd fix the ceremony if I could get the bride and family up to Wigan.

The day came, an ambulance with white wedding ribbons arrived at the registry office and decamped Lawrence on a stretcher. Formalities over, the bride and groom were photographed by the paparazzi gathering at the ambulance doors. The next day the photo dominated the centre spread of the *Daily Mirror* with a cross-page caption 'The service that looked after its own'. It probably did me no harm with the Air Ministry (if they even knew I existed).

After national service I embarked on my first grand tour of Europe with school friend Ian Stuchbery, a war-surplus commando tent and my treasured Ford Anglia. As my father had forecast, we ran out of francs long before we reached Paris on the return leg and, starving from a constant diet of cheap baguettes and mineral water, sought out Ford's office there, as instructed. Cash replenished, we were offered a trip to Chartres with visiting grandees from the Detroit head office. At lunchtime, the chauffeur rightly suggested that we wouldn't want to eat with the visiting Americans in a grand restaurant and he took us to a prefab routière on a bombed site, where most of the customers were truck drivers. We enjoyed the first truly first-class meal of our lives – garlicky terrine and cold roast pork with fresh mayonnaise and a pichet of vin ordinaire. With the Anglia, we flew out and back between Lympne airfield in Kent and Le Touquet in Normandy. I don't think that's possible now.

Not many have a choice between Merton at Oxford and Clare at Cambridge. My goal had always been Cambridge, an elegantly beautiful city with a much more ascetic culture than

Oxford. Going up to college is a strangely relaxed experience. You haul your luggage, radio, record player and a book or two into the porter's lodge at Clare's Memorial Court across the Backs, collect the key to your rooms, bid your parents (who have proudly driven you there) a quick goodbye, unpack and wait to be summoned by someone/anyone, don your Clare gown for the first time and venture nervously into hall searching for friendly looking freshmen to sit with. In the meantime, you are left to find your way around, meet people, buy some books on your syllabus and be perplexed by the strange lack of formal reception procedures.

At that time Clare had more than its fair share of good looking minor public school boys, courtesy of the then Master, Sir Henry Thirkill, who clung on to the admissions brief himself, resisting reforms that might broaden the diversity of undergraduates or college fellows (although Clare had some very bright grammar school boys.) I got to know Thirkill better when wealthy philanthropist Paul Mellon, who had been at Yale and Clare in the 1930s and endowed the Mellon Fellowships between them (one of which I was fortunate enough to enjoy) asked me to escort the elderly Sir Henry to America. For the Master of a Cambridge college, Sir Henry was remarkably unassertive. The metropolitan police magistrate Sybil Campbell once told me that he had been her physics supervisor at Cambridge, and was so shy with women that she had to conduct the sessions herself. His diffidence was balanced by some charismatic, far-thinking tutors at Clare.

Mr – later Sir – Geoffrey Elton, who was to be my Director of Studies in History, didn't approve of students doing National Service before university. They had, he insisted, lost the habit of study, or perhaps become less impressionable.

During an extremely uncomfortable interview with him, my total unsuitability for historical research was, quite justifiably, made plain.

Happily, a radical young don, Bill Wedderburn, Director of Studies in Law, found me in the Old Court looking down in the mouth. "What's the matter?" he asked. When I told him that I'd just seen Mr Elton, he replied: "Oh no, not another," and suggested I read law instead. Without any more ado, I walked with him across the Old Court and became a law student. I owe a great deal to Bill, who opened the door to my eventual career.

Bill was a brilliant Director of Studies, given to lamenting that we should have known him a year or two earlier when he was really ferocious. He had floppy, lanky hair over a pale rather intense face, and his wife Nina (granddaughter of the Victorian artist and feminist Nina Salaman) had floppy, lanky hair over a pale rather intense face. When you were invited to supper with Bill and Nina, you sat down at the table with their lodger, Jonathan Miller, a member of the Footlights satirical drama group, later a leading performer in *Beyond the Fringe* on the London stage, and an inventive actor and opera director as well as a doctor.

Unsurprisingly, that marriage was not to last, and Bill was later to marry the equally academic but less intense Dorothy Cole and then, to their mutual happiness, the non-academic but life-giving Frances. Bill claimed to be very left-wing but advised the Amalgamated Engineering Union, not very leftish at the time. He became a life peer, Lord Wedderburn of Charlton, for his work on company and labour law. His reforming *The Worker and the Law*, on what had been known as 'master and servant' law, was published by Penguin, and had been commissioned by Charles Clark, later our copyright consultant at the (book) Publishers Association.

I grew close to Bill, who was responsible for my being awarded the Mellon Fellowship at Yale even though I was in a state of nervous disability in the third year when preparing for my finals. On my return from Yale, Bill found me a pupillage in top chambers and, when I was group labour adviser at IPC, I drew on his advice. He conducted seminars for IPC managers on the controversial Tory Industrial Relations Act. Fleet Street, he told me once, had opened his eyes to the fact that not all unions were saintly.

Even in the unsympathetic Fifties, Bill was totally relaxed about me being gay. My supposed lover had dumped me, disastrously, after a happy summer on the grounds he was planning to be an Anglican cleric, and being gay was totally unacceptable. It took me a long time to recover. Looking back, how naïve I was, in tolerant Cambridge of all places. Bill sent me to see the tame college psychiatrist, which only made things worse. The psychiatrist settled me in the traditional leather chair (no couch), looked at me and proclaimed: "You have only one chance to change or you will be like it for life. Get yourself a girlfriend". (Hardly an easy task at Cambridge in the Fifties, even if I had been so inclined). Bill was aghast when I told him. He had asked the psychiatrist to tell me there were many others like me at Cambridge – and everywhere. It was, inevitably, a long time before I had another lover.

Law study at Cambridge was not unduly demanding. Unlike Yale Law School, the course was designed more as an academic exercise than as preparation for legal practice. Many barristers did not study it as undergraduates, opting for history, PPE or classics. At Cambridge we did lots of Roman law, history of law and constitutional law, essential and valuable knowledge, but no company or family law, with crime the main areas of practice in many barristers' chambers. Bill taught us basic contract and tort at weekly supervisions. He was really a corporate law specialist, and didn't give university lectures to undergraduates. Other supervisors varied in their eccentricity and niceness (H Whaley Tooker) or dryness (Henry Wade). Luckily, some young practitioners, down from the bar at weekends to earn a much-needed crust, brought a dose of reality to our studies.

Law lectures were held in the historic Old Schools, just across the lane from Clare. The schedule we delinquents followed was to attend the 10am lecture, have coffee at the Whim at 11am, take the midday lecture and abscond to the Bath pub at 1pm. There were textbooks to fill the gaps, along with the weekly schedule of five supervisions and five essays. Actually, I worked quite hard and well until the traumas of the third year.

In that year, I had gorgeous rooms in the Old Court over the main gate, with oriel windows at front and back. It should have been idyllic, but trying to read *Wade* [the other one] on *Real Property*, while in a state of deep depression, with the sights and sounds of undergraduates and tourists enjoying themselves under my windows, was beyond me.

Surprisingly, I was not a great one for extra-curricular activity at Cambridge, no student journalism or acting, two-player squash for sport, and I was hardly aware of the Bumps boat races on the Cam. I did contribute to, though not compete in, the Union. As an activist in student politics, I eschewed Labour to support the Liberals, but blotted my copybook during the Suez crisis, impetuously defending the invasion to my fellow students over breakfast in my second year digs. Stuck with the reputation of being an Anthony Eden supporter, I kept away from further political activity.

Looking back, I can begin to understand my viewpoint. The Suez Canal was then owned and operated by the United Kingdom and France, both still significant powers, and was a crucial shortcut for trade with the Far East. Colonel Nasser, Egypt's revolutionary President, was seen as the irresponsible enemy. Even so, I was on the wrong side of history. I recovered my faith in Labour (if not religion) at Yale, where the Congregationalist chaplain William Sloane Coffin, a prominent anti-racist campaigner, was a good friend.

My co-Mellon from Clare, David Caplin, school friend Ian Stuchbery and I crossed the Atlantic, steerage class, in the SS *United States*. We were met at the New York dockside by Michael Henchman, a Mellon Fellow who stayed at Yale a third year to complete his doctorate. He drove us back to our unfurnished college rooms and introduced us to our first American meal at the United Greece, otherwise known inevitably as the Greasy Spoon, a 24-hour Greek cafe where you lifted your feet up so the cleaner could mop the floor, putting us students firmly in our place. The food was decent and cheap. Michael became a much valued friend.

After the rather spartan regime at Clare, life at Berkeley College was almost luxurious. I had a bed-sitting room looking out on the Sterling Library and the Cross-Campus. I shared a bathroom with three or four undergraduates, made more tricky by the room doors which would slam shut – and lock. If you didn't have your key, you would find yourself stranded in the hallway in the Connecticut winter wearing only a towel, relying on a friend to run across to the Porter's Lodge to get a spare. Meals at Berkeley were self-service in a grand pseudo-Gothic hall, and Yalies didn't suffer inferior food gladly.

One of the original purposes of the Mellon Fellowships was for Clare graduates to help develop the Oxbridge college system at Yale. My personal contribution was to direct, very badly, college amateur dramatics, including the traditional skit *Murder in the Red Barn*, T S Eliot's *Murder in the Cathedral*, and an atrocious musical version I wrote of *The Country Wife*, for which the (much better) music and lyrics were written by Bill Weeden and David Finkle, who both became well-known in the Manhattan theatre. (David became drama critic for *Village Voice*, and Bill a successful actor.) I played Mrs Pinchwife, but the concept of a pantomime dame was unfortunately unknown in America at the time.

Bill Coffin, or more respectfully the Reverend William Sloane Coffin, born into a distinguished Mayflower family, who led civil rights demonstrations to the southern states, invited me to occasional dinners, introducing me to his father-in-law, the distinguished pianist Arthur Rubinstein. I founded a new society for seniors (final fourth year students) in Berkeley College, the Commonplace Society, named after the 'commonplace' book compiled by Bishop Berkeley, after whom the college was named. We met in the Master's Lodge on Sunday evenings with papers by a senior undergraduate or college fellow, followed by discussion and whiskey sours. Many years later, I was delighted to receive a copy of the Yale College magazine celebrating the Commonplace Society's fiftieth anniversary.

The most valuable part of my time at Yale was supposed to be at Yale Law School, one of the world's most distinguished law faculties. This didn't work out well. When I signed in on arrival, I said I was to take the basic or first law course, the Ll.B. in two years rather than three, claiming a year's credit for my degree from Cambridge. The registrar looked doubtful, saying that Professor Myres Macdougal, Dean of Graduate Students, would never allow this as I had already taken a degree at Cambridge. I protested that Yale's degree, designed to train practising lawyers, was very different from Cambridge's academic course. Yale's degree also offered me, I pointed out, a potentially lucrative practice in Anglo-American litigation. All this cut no ice, so I was put down for a Ll.M, a course principally designed to train law teachers.

I signed up for some intriguing rather highbrow courses on various aspects of jurisprudence with some brilliant tutors, but did not have a faculty member as supervisor. This disparate collection of seminars would be of questionable value in my intended career at the English bar. Only two professors showed much interest. One was the great legal philosopher F S C Northrop, who specialised in comparative international law (with a particular emphasis on South East Asia) and an ardent advocate of the need to understand local cultures deeply when you dealt with them. Obvious but too seldom followed. The other was Passerin d'Entrèves, a nomadic Italian scholar – he taught at Bologna, Oxford and Yale term by term – who specialised in political thought and natural law. These two at least gave me 'A's for my occasional papers, whereas Bayless Manning, Alexander Bickel and the other brilliant scholars didn't give me much personal attention. While he was at Yale, Passerin gave me the occasional lunch at the Graduate Club, and treated me to some challenging conversations.

I should have protested and requested a supervisor. As a graduate, I had little contact with the general run of students, or with those on my course, ambitious potential law teachers or politicians from friendly countries in Asia. I dreaded my lonely evenings high up in the dark stacks of the law library, reading mind-destroying articles, law reports and textbooks under a single light bulb in my carrel, or feeling like an outcast in the law school dining hall, when Berkeley College was much more welcoming.

Inevitably, I spent less and less time on my course, devoting more time to Berkeley and my interest in American politics and culture in Washington and Manhattan. When I visited New Haven years later, the Law School still struck me as unwelcoming. The marvellous – architectural and literary – Beinecke Rare Book and Manuscript Library, the Yale Center for British Art and the Elizabethan Club, of which I was and am a member, housed in a fine New England clapboard house, with both senior and junior members of the university, celebrating British art and literature, serving tea and wine, with a large safe filled with precious antiquarian books, especially Shakespearean originals.

Years later, I received my copy of the *Yale Law School Journal*, and saw that it contained a 'festschrift' (a book in honour) devoted to the retiring Professor Macdougal, proclaiming that he was the only person known to have been awarded three first – or equivalent – law degrees, from Mississippi, Oxford and Yale. (I suspect this was an affectionate joke at his expense since he was certainly something of a degree hunter). Macdougal's special student was the brilliant Ros Cohen, a contemporary from Cambridge, an international lawyer who, as Dame the Lady Ros Higgins, became the first woman president of the International Court of Justice at The Hague. Ros and I had a happy friendship attending Yale social events, Ros was engaged, at least in principle, to Terence Higgins, later a Tory MP and minister, and me not exactly looking for a girlfriend.

In spite of my disenchantment with Yale Law School, I had a tremendous time at Yale, with a circle of friends, some still in touch. Sociable late night cokes at George and Harry's. Intense, rather camp, drama rehearsals. Regular free cinema visits with Harald Tusberg, a Norwegian friend who had starred as the leading sea cadet, up the masts and all, in the blockbuster ultra-wide screen movie *Windjammer*. (Harald later ran NRK, Norway's state broadcaster).

The highlight was a three-month tour across the US and Mexico with David Caplin, staying with wealthy Yale parents (spending days at their country clubs), with less exalted individuals from the Committee for Friendly Relations with Foreign Students, or in grotty motels that might have provided the model for Norman Bates's establishment in *Psycho*.

David earned my undying admiration when, in Atlanta, we were asked if we would go to church on Sunday with our hosts. Of course we agreed, not realising that a Church of God Sunday service lasted all day. As proceedings ended with discussion and prayers, David politely asked why there were no black people in the congregation.

After two years of National Service, three years at Cambridge, two at Yale, and my bar finals, I abandoned my position as a pupil in chambers and joined the BBC. As Professor Glanville Williams had warned at Cambridge, in those days you needed a private income to see you through the long years before you could expect to earn a living at the bar.

Interlude
PAUL MELLON

I HAD IMMENSE good fortune in getting a Mellon Fellowship giving me two privileged years at Yale University in New Haven, Connecticut. The fellowship was endowed by Paul Mellon, the American philanthropist and art collector. Paul was the son of Andrew Mellon, a billionaire who created a vast business empire at the end of the nineteenth century and beginning of the twentieth, serving as Treasury Secretary under Presidents Harding, Coolidge and Hoover, in the run up to the Wall Street Crash and the Great Depression.

Paul inherited his wealth. He and his father donated their magnificent art collections to America's National Gallery, alternatively called the Mellon Gallery. Paul donated a second collection to the Yale Center for British Art in New Haven. He was a generous benefactor to Yale University and Clare College.

With no great interest in running the extensive Mellon business, Paul must have been the total opposite of his father. To me, he was a typical sophisticated courteous New Englander, although his main home was in Virginia, at Oak Spring in Upperville. His second wife, Bunny, was a renowned gardener and horticulturist who designed the Oak Spring Gardens and the Rose Garden at the White House. I fear we didn't fully appreciate her talent when she showed us the gorgeous gardens at Oak Spring, which she turned into a national treasure.

My first visit was in 1959 when I, and my fellow-Mellon Fellow David Caplin, who was reading physics at the Yale Graduate School (he was to become a distinguished eminent professor of low temperature physics at Imperial College), were invited to lunch with

INTERLUDE

Paul and Bunny. We were advised that it was expected that, while in Washington, we should call on him at his Virginia home. We could expect an enjoyable lunch and an opportunity to show our gratitude. We went to Oak Spring on a glorious Sunday in April.

Between us, we had bought an old Ford principally for our summer driving around the United States (we wrote it off in Kentucky, leaving me with a repaired, but still bent, nose.) and drove deep into Virginia. We were in something of a quandary as to what we could take to convey our appreciation of the generous fellowship. Given that our host was one of the wealthiest people in the world, and we couldn't afford a small Picasso, we needed something beautiful and symbolic. We settled on a small, exquisite plant, possibly an azalea.

The butler, who greeted us at the front door, remarked how pleased Mrs Mellon would be – her favourite plant, he said – took the pot and asked us to wait a moment. He returned with our plant in a gorgeous silver bowl, which he held aloft as he led us into the drawing room, where Paul and Bunny and assorted guests met us, praising our offering which did look rather splendid on the windowsill, bathed in sunlight.

The first great pre-lunch ritual was the making of the martinis, a task undertaken by Paul, with his butler passing over the ingredients. An entire bottle of excellent gin was poured into a jug of ice-cubes, and immediately poured off into another jug into which a suspicion of martini was added. No olives, no sliver of zest, just chilled and lightly-flavoured strong gin, served in a Waterford tumbler. I had never tasted a dry martini before, and this one was absolutely delicious, disappearing rather rapidly. Paul was – I suspect – an amused onlooker. "You obviously enjoyed that, Clive. Would you like another?" Another tumbler of dry – very dry – martini was duly delivered.

PAUL MELLON

Lunch passed in a haze. There was a waiter behind each chair – well, behind mine, anyway – and the food was superb, although neither large nor absorbent. As all the other guests declined the butler's offer of second helpings, I felt I couldn't indulge and be the last one eating. Luckily, I didn't seem to be expected to talk. Presumably, David covered for me.

I don't remember much more until, over coffee, Bunny Mellon mercifully asked whether, as I obviously liked plants, I would like to see the garden. Apparently the main garden outside the house was a replica of the French Gardens at Versailles, based on Louis XV's historic Petit Trianon.

Along the walls of the orangerie were *trompe l'oeil* paintings depicting what was behind them in each cupboard: spades, forks, hoes, twine, bulbs, seeds, gourds. And the orangerie was full of azaleas (or whatever it was we'd brought). "I'm so glad you like them, Clive," Bunny said, "they really are my favourites at this time of the year, as you can see."

A couple of years later, when I was a BBC producer, living with flatmates in Kensington, I got an invitation to visit the United States again. One evening the phone rang and the caller said he was Paul Mellon. "Come off it," I said, "who are you?" It took some time to convince me that this wasn't a hoax. Transatlantic calls, let alone from billionaires, were unusual back then.

Paul had found out that Sir Henry Thirkill, the senior tutor when he was at Clare (since retired as Master, and well over 80 with a heart condition) had never been to America. Paul wanted to rectify this, but 'Thirks' would need an escort. "Would I be happy to take this on, with all my expenses paid?"

My BBC department head gave me leave, even arranging an add-on business trip to meet executives of the Canadian Broadcasting Corporation in Toronto. A few weeks later, I found myself in economy class in a VC10 to Idlewild airport (now JFK). To, I guess, our mutual relief, Sir Henry travelled up front.

We stayed for several days in Yale as Sir Henry and I called on Whitney Griswold, the university president, Gene Rostow, the dean of the law school, and the Sterling librarian. We went daily to the Elizabethan Club (the Lizzy) to meet the current Mellon Fellows and some undergraduates and teachers and view the fine collection of Elizabethan books, including Shakespeare folios and first editions of Milton's *Paradise Lost*, Spenser's *Faerie Queene*, and Bacon's *Essayes*.

From New Haven we flew to Upperville in Mellon's private jet. The highlight of the visit came when Paul gave us a personal tour of the big house, where his father had lived but which he didn't like. This was where he stored the pictures which were later given to the Washington National Gallery and the Yale Center for British Art. In rooms furnished with racks hung with paintings, Paul showed us some favourite pieces. We were accompanied by Basil Taylor, his British buyer, who was nearly blind by then but so trusted that he had a virtually unlimited budget to enhance the collections.

On the last day, the butler found me in the gardens and told me that Mr Mellon would like to see me. Slightly nervous at the headmaster-style summons, I was shown to the study where, over coffee, I was briefed on our upcoming visits to Washington and New York City. With no hint of irony, Paul warmly thanked me for giving my time to the visit, adding that he hoped that looking after Sir Henry wasn't proving too onerous.

And then came the big question from one of the world's wealthiest men: "How are you off for money, Clive?" Fortunately, as a well-brought up polite young Englishman, I replied. "Oh, fine, thank you, sir".

He didn't ask a second time, but he did say that in Washington (Hays-Adams House) and New York (Yale Club), I shouldn't hesitate to charge dinner and other expenses to his accounts. Although duly grateful, I asked myself whether, when the bills arrived, I could really say "That's all right; my good man, just send it to Paul Mellon", so we avoided the more expensive eateries. I realise now that I should have asked his secretary to arrange it.

In Washington DC, Paul had arranged for us to be given a personal tour of the National Gallery by the director, John Walker. Sir Henry was put in a wheelchair, and off we went. Mr Walker had selected 15 or so of his favourite paintings and arranged for the appropriate curator to talk us through each masterpiece. I can't imagine a more rewarding way of learning how to look at a painting.

Sir Henry didn't much like New York city and I had to get him off the viewing platform of the Empire State Building in a hurry. I dispatched him back to London from Idlewild, and he arrived safely in Cambridge, only slightly worse for wear. When I returned to Cambridge to report back to Sir Eric Ashby, Clare's new Master, 'Thirks' told me he had found the trip "memorable", as well he might.

Chapter 2:
My father, Alfred Bradley

MY FATHER, ALFRED BRADLEY, made the unfortunate mistake of dying during the national newspaper strike which, extraordinarily, took place during the 1970 General Election, thereby denying himself a well-deserved obituary, and getting me into some trouble to boot.

That was the election in which Prime Minister Harold Wilson, having been defeated by his Home Secretary Jim Callaghan in his battle to reform industrial relations with his *In Place of Strife* strategy, unexpectedly lost to Edward Heath. Wilson later made the mistake of resigning as Prime Minister in such a way as to favour Callaghan as his successor, making way not only for an older man but for someone who had diminished his place in history, declaring at Harold's farewell party that "history will think better of you than your contemporaries". Why SOGAT leader Bill Keys thought a newspaper strike during the campaign would help Labour (assuming he did), was always beyond me.

I was Deputy General Manager of the *Daily* and *Sunday Mirror* when my father died, and thought that, since I had very little to do during the strike, which was being negotiated at Newspaper Publishers Association level, my place was with my mother, arranging the funeral.

My father did at least three notable things. He was the first businessman anywhere, as early as 1951, to invest big money in a computer (LEO) designed for office rather than scientific or military use. He invented PAYE, or at least the coding system, for income tax. He planted the seed that led to one-day first class cricket. On the other side, he had all Ford's typewriters, thousands of them, converted to 'all caps'. This possibly unauthorised decision was designed to implement an Operations & Methods report (much favoured at the time) which concluded that 20 percent of typists' efforts (then on manual typewriters) was taken up pressing the shift key for a capital letter. Logically, therefore, if letters could be typed in 'all caps', typists would be 20 percent more productive. Unfortunately, this failed to acknowledge that reading text relies more on word-shape recognition than on actual spelling, and 'all cap' words look very similar. After his retirement the typewriters were converted back to upper and lower case.

Only at the funeral did I learn of his role in pioneering PAYE during the war. His former boss and chairman of Ford, Sir Roland Smith, told me the story at the wake. During the war, tax levels rose to such an extent that blue collar workers, who had previously been exempt – unless perhaps, they were Fleet Street linotype operators – were becoming liable for tax. The unions, of course, were against this, and argued that you could not expect relatively low-paid manual workers to save enough during the year to pay their annual taxes in the two existing tranches, in January and July. Nor, they argued, could tax be deducted from the weekly pay packet at source because requiring workers to disclose their private family arrangements for their liability to be assessed would be a gross invasion of privacy.

My father, then working half a week at Dagenham and the other half at the Ministry of Supply, was invited to join the Inland Revenue Committee, chaired by Sir Paul Chambers, to consider this intractable problem. He went away quietly to come and devised the coding system which we still have today, specifying the necessary deduction to be made without disclosing any personal details. Understandably he preferred to keep quiet about this substantial contribution to modern life.

His role in commissioning LEO has featured in books on the history of the computer, a joint project between Joe Lyons (John Simmons) and Ford (Alfred Bradley) to develop a computer to handle routine office systems – the Lyons Electronic Office. My father contributed Ford's cash and the conviction that computers, then massive things grinding out scientific data in laboratories, could transform office work, payrolls and stock control. He told me about his plans on our evening walks. Ironically, when I joined the book industry in 1976, publishers, with their stocks of book titles, like car makers with spare parts, were still struggling with their reliance on human input. We did something to help through the development of automated electronic teleordering between retailers, wholesalers and publishers' warehouses.

Actually the books on LEO don't do my father justice. The most detailed, published by McGraw Hill in the USA, describes my father as 'Mr Bradley' because no-one, they told me, apparently knew the first name of this quiet man behind the successful development of LEO.

The one-day cricketing story showed similar persistence. Having visited Ford in the United States several times and been entertained at the Detroit Tigers' baseball stadium at Comerica Park, my father was impressed by the system in baseball by which teams alternate batting after three 'outs' so that the spectators have a good chance to see both sides and their star players. He was infuriated that only being able to watch county games and Test matches on Saturdays – there was no play on Sundays at the time – he would often see only one team bat. If Australia batted second, he might never get to see the great Donald Bradman. His campaign, backed by the *Evening News*, met with a frosty reception from the nawabs of Lord's. Cricket was psychological, they apparently argued, and the full three or five days was needed to play itself out. But the seed was sown, and he lived to see at least the first one day games. I do, though, sometimes wonder how he'd regard today's 20:20s.

My father's background was not humble, but nor was it charmed. His father, Isaac Bradley was a moderately well-off man, apparently from a scrap metal business in Manchester during the First World War, who left all but a handful of rent-controlled slum houses to his first family. My father was the youngest child in the second. Isaac was also a firm believer in the University of Life, and insisted that Alfred, although obviously intelligent, left school at 15 to work in the cotton industry. Studying at evening classes, my father qualified as a Chartered Secretary and became an Associate of the Institute of Chartered Secretaries and Administrators. (He resigned in protest at the Institute's failure to grant Fellowships to members who were not actually company secretaries, no matter how eminent they were.) He did well enough in his examinations to be asked to teach – evenings only – at the adult college where he had studied.

After joining Ford at Trafford Park he rose quickly enough to be left in charge of closing the Manchester plant and the move to Dagenham, where he became Director of Administration, a safe pair of hands for the giant car, truck and tractor manufacturer's wartime management problems. He retired in 1960, soon after the American company took full control of the business, something he did not appreciate.

Like many of his age, my father volunteered to enlist in the Army at the premature age of 17, in 1915, and would have fought in the trenches if he had not caught pneumonia during training on Salisbury Plain, leading to a spell in the Military Hospital on Millbank, clerical work at the War Office, and then a return to work in Manchester. There, perhaps something of a hard-working recluse, taking a lone holiday cruise in the Mediterranean he met my mother, marrying her in 1928. Their elder child, Pauline Anne, was born in Manchester in 1931. They moved to Upminster in 1933 where, a year later, I joined the family. We moved from a suburban house in Corbets Tey Road to a grand villa, splendidly named Aidacra (Arcadia backwards) in Hall Lane, Upminster's top residential road.

As retiring empty nesters, they moved to Hove in 1961, living there until 1970, when my father died of a massive heart attack on a solo practice round on the golf course. In Hove, he pottered in the small greenhouse, walked on the promenade, and enjoyed the local cricket ground, especially a splendid spat with the local cricket club secretary who objected to his leaving his car overnight near the boundary to guarantee a prime spot the following day. At his funeral, Congregational minister, Emrys Walters, a friend (and a football commentator for the BBC), described him, with considerable understatement, as "the salt of the earth".

My father was a quiet man who achieved a lot, mostly unacknowledged. Probably not one of the world's great lovers, but an affectionate husband who balanced a demanding work life with a remarkably active social life. There were enjoyable family outings to Westcliff and Southend pier, delightful holidays in Henley during the war (punting, muddy swims and dreadful food) and Broadstairs at Braeside, a small hotel run by the friendly religious Misses Chisholm, my father leading me excitedly in our dressing gowns to before-breakfast swims in the icy water at Dumpton Gap. Pauline met her future husband David there. We managed to squeeze in three visits a fortnight to the Seaside Follies show (which changed programmes on Wednesdays), visiting Fortes Ice Cream Parlour where we were forbidden anything more expensive than a North (raspberry) or South (chocolate, or maybe *vice versa*) Pole. I was over sixty before I had my first Knickerbocker Glory, which didn't look anywhere near as glorious as the Fortes' monstrosities. My mother delighted in asking teachers and matrons and boys I did not particularly like to join us on these holidays, but I managed.

And underneath? Well, my father was proud of Pauline and myself, sending my sister to, of all things, a finishing school in Switzerland for a year in lieu of university (had she gone to university, who knows what she might have achieved), and giving me pocket money throughout my time at Cambridge, leaving me affluent enough to offer a sherry and throw the occasional party. And he gave me a retired Ford test car, for my eighteenth birthday, which saw me through National Service and Cambridge.

When he died, his bank manager greeted me with the words:"I hope you don't think your father was a wealthy man". Indeed he turned out not to be. Even senior managers were not well paid in those days and he had wanted to lead, and share, an enjoyable life. He left my mother adequately off, although with little surplus, and she was to live another 20 years in reasonable comfort.

I can't conclude this chapter without telling two stories

which vividly illustrate his personality. The first occurred soon after the introduction of parking meters in Hove. My father got his first ticket – a penalty of £1 or something – but insisted that it was a two-headed meter and as he'd inserted his sixpence in the wrong side, he had paid and therefore wasn't at fault. I told him he'd be wasting his time and should pay up, but he insisted on going to defend himself at the Magistrates' Court. I told him again that he didn't have a chance – the hearing would be routine, he wouldn't be believed, and he'd end up paying double. But he had time on his hands so along he went, sitting there while appellant after appellant making similar excuses was dealt with mercilessly. Perhaps he looked honest or perhaps the magistrates thought that, in the interests of justice being seen to be done, it was time to let someone off. I'll never forget the pleased smirk with which he told me.

Then he decided to buy a new car. He'd always had a Ford but this time wanted something different. So he bought a – very – second-hand Hillman Minx for £350, showing it off to me proudly. It took all of my acting ability to pretend not to see the prominent patches of rust on almost every part of the old banger. My parents set off to see Pauline in Devon in this monstrosity, somehow getting there but coming back in pouring rain with no windscreen wipers, oil pouring out everywhere, brakes dicey, and virtually every other mechanical part failing. His attempts to get the dealer to take the car back received the expected rebuffs. He sought my advice 'as a lawyer' and I reminded him, unsympathetically, of the legal maxim *caveat emptor*. Despite getting the same advice from an expensive counsel, he issued a writ himself and turned up at the County Court to press his claim.

The judge was less than patient, especially as my father

had been an executive in the motor industry, declaring that the court's time should not be taken up with such a sorry story. He gave the parties 30 minutes to settle the matter outside. The second-hand car dealer shrugged, smiled, and repaid the £350. "Call yourself a lawyer? I gave you an expensive education at Cambridge and Yale, had you called to the Bar, and I won the case against your advice without a minute of legal training. Huh!" Real pleasure!

The car he gave me on my eighteenth birthday had its own story. I'd walked past the local garage a few weeks before, proudly displaying my new driving licence to all and sundry, and there on display was a bull-nosed Morris, complete with dickey seat which folded out at the back. I knew that the car had had only one careful owner, old Mr Woollings, who drove it to church on Sundays. It was £50, and I had £50 in Barclays across the road – all I had in fact. Five minutes later I drove up Hall Lane to show my car to my mother. "No no", she cried, "you can't have that. Take it back at once, I'll phone Mr Aggiss and tell him to take it back". I thought she was being a mean old mum, fearful of her son driving his first car. It was years before I appreciated that she knew all about the forthcoming gift, and knew how disappointed my father would be if I had pre-empted it. Actually, a bull-nosed Morris would be worth a fortune today, but at least my father – and mother – knew what I wanted.

Chapter 3:

My mother, Kathleen Bradley

IF MY FATHER had the bad luck of dying during the 1970 newspaper strike, denying himself a decent obituary, my mother, Annie Kathleen (*née* Turner), who liked to be known as Kathleen or, in her later years when she was painting, Kay, had an equivalent, and much more serious, misfortune. Being born in 1895, she was just 18 when the First World War broke out, and only 22 when it ended, belonging to a generation of young women who suffered from the devastation inflicted on the country's young men.

My mother didn't marry until she was 32. Of her three younger sisters, Beth married a much older man, Douglas Scott-Mutlow, who seemed to have a small private income and was a past crony of their father, the Reverend Fred Willey Turner. Beth and Douglas settled in Newquay (lobster teas up the Gannel when you went to stay). Winifred, an accomplished old school nurse who, we were told, had been jilted by a surgeon when she was younger, remained single, leading a successful and strict career in private nursing at Great Ormond Street Hospital. The highlight of her work was being summoned to Buckingham Palace whenever the young princesses, Elizabeth and Margaret Rose, and later their children, were suffering childhood illnesses. Molly, the child of grandfather's second marriage, married Jack Chandler, a Customs official and dedicated botanist and philatelist. They had two boys, Richard, who became a professor of civil engineering (soil mechanics meaning quakes and dam bursts) at Imperial College, and Robin. Richard is a highly reputed ornithologist, author of some scholarly bird books with his own superb photos. His mother, Molly was a thoroughly modern young woman and a good musician, who died too young. The Chandler family would join us for many Christmases, bringing a massive pork pie from Spalding which we enjoyed over many breakfasts.

Pauline and I never got to know our father's family in Manchester that well, though we made regular family trips to see them. His eldest sister Dora married Tom Longan and had two successful, bright children, Sheila and Donald. Pauline and Dora never got on (probably because they shared the same characteristics). I spent enjoyable weekends with Dora and Tom when I was on National Service in Lancashire. I won a goldfish at a local fete which was apparently still alive twenty years later, surely deserving an entry in the *Guinness Book of Records*. Donald and I were contemporaries. We both had active careers which, although we had much in common, meant we didn't meet up as regularly as we would have liked. Donald was a senior manager in the construction industry and finished his career at Henley Research, the institute specialising in training for acquisition strategies for executives and talent.

The second sister Gertrude, married Bob Frost, and had a daughter Elaine. I stayed with them on family visits, sleeping on a camp bed in their hall under a grandfather clock which chimed every fifteen minutes, and was taken to see Manchester City, standing proudly on the terraces, frozen to death, barely able to see a thing. Bert, the third sibling, married Bella. They had three children, Pamela, Roy – and Alan, who was a heroically regular visitor to my mother.

Before my mother married, she was a successful journalist.

Her father, Fred Willey Turner, was a liberally-inclined Baptist minister born in Sheffield, who was funded through theological college by the deacons of his local chapel. My mother, his first child, was born in 1895 when he had a ministry in Pudsey, Yorkshire. His main ministry was in Evesham where he brought up the family, moving to the Hertfordshire village of Markyate at the end of his career where my mother, dressed as a flapper, and father, in conventional wedding rig, were married in a teetotal wedding in 1928.

My grandfather's first wife, our maternal grandmother Annie Marsh, died in middle age, and he married again – to Alice Watts, the headmistress of Dresden House, the local girls' school in Evesham, a decision that didn't go down too well with his daughters who were pupils there. He had a second career, as a columnist for the nonconformist weekly, the *Christian World*, writing regular features particularly during the First World War. He turned down the editorship of the *Christian World* in the possibly mistaken belief that his true vocation lay with the ministry. My mother inherited his journalistic bent, which was passed on to me and to my nephew, Jonathan – four generations in one family.

My mother was one of the relatively small number of women journalists in Fleet Street in the Twenties, moving from the *Evesham Journal*, where she had started out as a cub reporter, to the *Daily News* – later renamed the *News Chronicle* – in Manchester, and then to the London office. There she worked, as women journalists did then, largely on the women's pages, but she interviewed, amongst many others, Nancy Astor, Bernard Shaw and the painter William Orpen, who in response to her question as to what made women lovely, drew a self-portrait with a cartoon balloon saying. 'All women are lovely. Why worry?', which got top billing in her article. This plum assignment was given to her after she'd been accidentally caught up in a Fenian (pre-IRA) outrage, on which she filed an eye-witness report.

Back then it was not seen as proper for married women to have a career and so, even though some more liberal women did juggle both successfully, and despite a determined campaign by the NUJ, the managing director, Sir Egbert Cadbury of the Quaker family, insisted that she leave. Like so many women of her generation, she became a suburban housewife, expected to support her husband. In truth, she was hardly overcome by domestic chores, as we had a live-in young Irish maid, Rosie, to clean and do much of the cooking and a part-time nanny to look after the children. That may sound luxurious but losing her job in the prime of her journalistic career must have hurt. A life of suburban coffee and tea parties with other wives was a poor substitute. While she made some attempts at free-lance writing, and was once invited to appear on a quiz show in the early days of television at Alexandra Palace, it didn't really work out.

The Second World War was a time of new opportunity for such women. Certainly my mother, though not engaged in war work (but supporting a husband who very much was), found that going in her tin hat to the local Methodist hall, converted into a NAAFI, to make tea, coffee and snacks for the troops billeted locally, gave her a new lease of life.

In older age, while maintaining a good outgoing life, she found it increasingly difficult to be alone, and possibly unduly suspicious about the endless possibilities of father having dalliances with other women (which, if they occurred at all, certainly never threatened their marriage or their pleasant social life). In the Sixties, she showed a new interest in painting and pottery. I have some of her pictures which show real talent.

She lived for 20 more years after the death of my father, never enjoying a solitary life or finding a home where she felt happy. She had too much independence to enjoy the various homes she lived in, and too much dependence to be on her own. She was too demanding a presence to live with Pauline or myself, and she knew it. There was one dreadful period when well-meaning friends (and fellow painters) in Bognor persuaded her to rent a small bed-sitting room opposite their house, where she lived for a time with a coin-slot meter for her gas fire, sharing a kitchen and bathroom with an Iranian student of whom she was intensely suspicious. Before that she had lived in a tiny room in a small boarding house in Hove, magnificently looked after by the owners before they sold to a less helpful couple. We got her out of the Bognor flat into a succession of excellent Abbeyfield homes, but she was always lonely, no matter how often Pauline and I visited. As you get older yourself, you realise how brief and disturbing these short family visits can be. She would adopt the role of shop steward for the other residents, which actually won her more respect and affection from the staff than we feared might be the case.

She lived until she was 94, still spritely and anxious to play a full part in family life when she was visiting, driving her offspring scatty with her troublesome deaf aid and her inability to master its flat batteries, intervening inappropriately in conversations. But she had a good and long life and died on Pauline's fifty-ninth birthday. We thought it would be a pleasant gesture to ask the Congregational minister taking her funeral (who knew her quite well) to thank the Abbeyfield Extra-Care staff in Taunton for looking after a sometimes difficult resident.

He went further than we intended when he started the service by exceeding his brief about a woman who had, it appeared, been more difficult than most. All that said my mother was a caring and intelligent woman who made her mark and, at last, got a well-deserved obituary in the *Times*. The truth was that she never got over the price she paid for marriage - the abrupt termination of her career as a journalist. How little we know about our parents. How little we ask.

It occurs to me that, as we do with our parents, this account shows too little understanding. Looking at the picture of her at her wedding, in a short flapper dress, she was clearly something of a Bright Young Thing in the Twenties. She had been a reporter on the *Daily News* for some eight years, by any standards a glamorous - and for women at that time extremely rare - occupation, with lots of friends at work and evenings out. She lodged in North London, with the mother and father of a curate who became a high-flying bishop, providing a safe and welcoming base. This was to be replaced by suburban life, with a generous husband but one who had little appreciation (as I discovered) of a frivolous career journalist and perhaps some sibling jealousy. How she must have looked back on those golden years, not understood by either her husband or her children or her neighbours.

Chapter 4:

Bar and BBC

I WAS CALLED to the Bar by the Middle Temple in 1960 and was fortunate to be offered a pupillage in a distinguished set of commercial chambers, Brick Court, courtesy of Bill Wedderburn. If this had happened before I went to Yale, my pupil master would have been the successful barrister Sam Cooke, but during my absence he'd taken silk, and so couldn't take on pupils, and I was assigned to a junior barrister who I didn't take to.

My career as a barrister was beginning to look rather unpromising, influenced by Glanville Williams's dire warnings at Cambridge that you needed to have a private income to practice at the Bar, and because my father, who had very generously kept me in pocket in the RAF and at university, was anxious to retire on his not very generous Ford pension.

My doubts were strengthened by my renewed friendship with Christopher James, a contemporary at Felsted and Cambridge, who had just set himself up in chambers in the Inner Temple. As a lawyer's son, he knew all the ins and outs. After our first lunch, we were walking back down Middle Temple Lane, when an elderly gentleman, who turned out to be a High Court judge, called Christopher over for being improperly dressed because he wasn't wearing a bowler hat within the Temple. Having enjoyed the informality of America, I wasn't sure I could tolerate such a stuffy environment. So when Kenneth Lamb, chief assistant of current affairs (later head of religious broadcasting and

Secretary) of the BBC, called to ask if I would be interested in a graduate traineeship, I jumped at the chance. True, I was technically too old for the scheme but Kenneth assured me this could be overcome. The salary – £950 a year – was much higher than anything I could expect to earn at the Bar.

Was it sensible to turn my back on so many years' study? Probably not, but, on balance, it felt like the right decision. Many years later, flying back from the European Court of Justice with the Publishers Association's junior counsel, Stephen Richards (later a Lord Justice at the Court of Appeal), I wondered whether if I had stayed at the Bar, I might have been significantly better off. Stephen replied that, if anything, I was the person he envied most for having had such a fascinating range of jobs. He had, he said, devoted most of the previous six months to a tedious Japanese case on ball-bearing monopolies, relieved only by our much more interesting case at the ECJ. As my subsequent career involved a significant amount of litigation and legislation, I was classified anyway by the Bar Council as an 'employed barrister'.

Being incontrovertibly gay, I was also deeply aware of the 1961 movie *Victim*, starring Dirk Bogarde as a gay barrister facing extreme prejudice. If I needed any further encouragement to pursue a different career, that heart-breaking drama certainly provided it.

And so, a few days later, I found myself at the BBC with a desk in Bush House as a trainee radio producer in the North American service. My parents were probably relieved that at long last I was earning a salary. The BBC struck them as rather glamorous and they seemed disappointed that I wasn't on *Tonight* that very first evening when I unexpectedly arrived home for supper.

To be honest, I shared their disappointment. After Cambridge and Yale, the North American service felt like something of a backwater. Only later, during a second stint there as a regular current affairs producer, did I realise it was a plum training assignment. The department head, George Steedman, was a terrifying, brilliant, mentor, who tore our programmes apart at his weekly playback session. Afterwards, we were picked up from the floor by his able deputy, Christopher Bell.

A few weeks after I joined, I was asked to act as 'uncle' to two new graduate trainees, Melvyn Bragg and Philip Whitehead, who would both enjoy remarkably distinguished careers. Melvyn became *the* arts presenter, a novelist and a life peer while Philip, a senior producer on *Panorama* and *This Week*, excelled as MP, MEP, and chair of the Consumers' Association and Fabian Society. Their first training assignments were in the overseas talks and features department. Another trainee who enjoyed a successful broadcasting career and became a lifelong friend was John Miller, who rashly became part of a consortium to win the commercial franchise for TV South, a hanging offence at the BBC in those days. John was not only a successful television producer, he wrote well-received biographies of theatrical eminences like John Gielgud, Judi Dench, Ralph Richardson and Peter Ustinov, served as artistic director of the Winchester Arts Festival and produced a series of events for me at the Publishers Association, including a literary festival in Westminster Abbey.

Bush House was known as an exceptionally pleasant place to work. It was full of charismatic writers from different cultures which received BBC European and overseas broadcasts (who to the benefit of us all, including that of invading academics from the London School of Economics across the road, demanded a good canteen), and trainees were actually allowed to make programmes. At the North American service, the intellectual elite included Barbara Halpern (a niece of Lytton Strachey), culture guru Philip French, military historian John Terraine, children's author Gordon Snell (who married Irish writer Maeve Binchy) and Trevor MacDonald, later to be a celebrated newsreader.

During training, I was assigned to *Today* and *Ten O'Clock*, BBC Radio's leading current affairs and news programmes. Jack de Manio presented *Today* under Betty Rowley's editorship, while Stephen Bonarjee ran *Ten O'Clock*, with various household-names presenting. On Bonarjee's show, trainees usually did nothing more demanding than meet interviewees at reception. On *Today*, which had a much bigger audience, we enjoyed more leeway. Occasionally, I even acted as sole producer, albeit with De Manio, who was famous for announcing the time incorrectly, keeping an eye on me.

In that exalted role, I was collected by limo at 3am, impressing the porters at Chelsea Cloisters, where I had a tiny flat, who assumed that I must have been embarking on an errand of global political significance. Actually all I had to do was stick to the prescribed running order, but I thought there could be no harm in showing some initiative. Once, I was impressed by a lovely piece I had heard on *Ten O'Clock* on the Amazon jungle. (I like to think it involved a young David Attenborough, whose career I would therefore have kick-started, but sadly the timelines don't add up.) Keen for the story to reach a much wider audience, I ordered the news tape from the library and inserted it into the *Today* programme, with no objection from Jack.

When I got back to the office, the atmosphere was frosty. Apart from deviating from the prescribed running order, apparently I had unknowingly blundered into a long-standing territorial dispute between the news and current affairs departments. Luckily, my initiative was interpreted as a triumph for current affairs (of which *Today* was part) and department head George Camacho sent me a congratulatory memo.

I was disappointed to be sent back to Bush House for my first regular position until I realised we were in a kind of holding camp for BBC2, the new TV channel which was about to come on air. My work included producing a weekly current affairs programme, *Call from London*, aimed at the North American radio market which was supplied with programme tapes sent by airmail. Usually presented by Erskine Childers (grandson of the author of *Riddle of the Sands* who had been executed as a traitor by the Irish in the 1920s), *Call from London* gave me virtual carte blanche to invite almost any guest I wanted. Our invitations were invariably accepted – interviewees from Fleet Street and Westminster were paid £15 for little trouble – and we attracted leading academics, journalists and politicians, such as Denis Healey, Dick Crossman, Jeremy Thorpe and Iain Macleod.

The political atmosphere at the time was intense. Edward Heath, not yet Prime Minister, was pursuing his unsuccessful negotiations to join the European Common Market, in defiance of Charles de Gaulle's 'Non'. In the wake of Harold Macmillan's 'Wind of Change' speech, many colonial independence negotiations, led by Macleod, were underway at nearby Lancaster House. I lugged my hefty tape recorder over there to interview such notable black leaders, hitherto regarded as treasonable insurgents, as Jomo Kenyatta (Kenya), Joshua Nkomo (Southern Rhodesia, now Zimbabwe), Kenneth Kaunda (Northern Rhodesia, now Zambia), Milton Obote (Uganda),

Julius Nyerere (Tanganyika, now Tanzania), Grantley Adams (Barbados, who had a son living at the Bede House foundation in Rotherhithe where I was a volunteer), and the acerbic Eric Williams (Trinidad). The South African crisis, with expulsion from the Commonwealth imminent, kept us up at night as the would they/wouldn't they drama unfolded.

Somewhere in the archives, there must be library tapes of my radio broadcasts with Eric Ashby, then the new Master of Clare College, on his momentous report on universal primary education in Nigeria. There must also be a record somewhere of a programme with Alun Gwynne-Jones, the *Times's* defence correspondent, on the peaceful uses of an army in international crises, now a much more regular occurrence. I introduced Alun to Harold Wilson, and, as Lord Chalfont, he was appointed a Foreign Office minister.

All this surprisingly led to my next career move when Denis Healey invited me to leave the BBC and become broadcasting officer of the Labour party ahead of the 1964 general election. For a politically ambitious young man, this was too good an opportunity to ignore. Without much thought – or indeed protest from my BBC bosses – I accepted.

My departure to Labour earned a mild rebuke from Grace Wyndham Goldie, the fearsome head of current affairs television, who told me (maybe truthfully) that I had been her first choice for BBC2. Luckily, this did not affect our subsequent relationship. Her doubts were understandable. Labour may well have chosen me because I was cheap and not well-known enough to rock the boat. The growing power of television was yet to be appreciated by many politicians.

When I received the invitation, Hugh Gaitskell was the Labour leader. While I worked out my notice at the BBC,

Gaitskell fell ill and died (for many years, it was suspected, wrongly, that he had been murdered by the Soviets). After a few anxious weeks in which my future hung in abeyance, new party leader Harold Wilson seemed happy and I joined Labour's staff on May Day, 1963.

I returned to the BBC in 1965, after my spell with Labour, as a production assistant on *Panorama*. There were obvious doubts about my impartiality. I spent a period of purdah in the presentation gallery, looking after continuity between programmes, a tightly controlled to-the-second exercise. I was in charge of the gallery for the day-long broadcast of Winston Churchill's funeral in January 1965.

As political editor of the *Statist*, I could take on broadcasts as a freelance, writing and delivering five-minute commentaries after the overseas news bulletins, and becoming an established panel member on the Overseas Service's coverage of Budgets and General Elections. For the first General Election of 1974, we went off air at about 2.30am, when the result was on a knife edge. In my turn to round-up, as the left-leaning journalist on the panel, I forecast that Wilson would come back as Prime Minister. Afterwards, the head of BBC Overseas Talk and Features reprimanded me for bias towards Labour, but I was right – I had just talked with the Liberal leader Jeremy Thorpe, whose support was needed to form a government with a voting majority, and knew he would never serve in any coalition led by Heath.

For two years, I hosted the weekly overseas programme *Business and Industry*. I was called in on a Sunday morning to present an emergency edition when the Labour Government had been forced to devalue the pound – the famous time when Harold Wilson was scorned for saying: "the pound in your pocket is still a pound". When I arrived in the studio, I found that my intended interviewees were still locked in Downing Street at a press conference. Producer Brian Sharp took the lead as presenter with me as sole interviewee. After about ten minutes, he whispered that the speakers had arrived and left me to keep on talking as he went into the cubicle to brief them. Somehow I ad libbed for about twenty minutes, only for Brian to forget to sign me off when he returned to close the programme.

ACT 2
PARTY
POLITICS

Interlude
THE 1964 ELECTION

IN 1963, THE next general election, due by October 1964, looked like a sure thing for Labour. The Conservatives had been in power since 1951, the Prime Minister Harold Macmillan, while reasonably popular with the public, had played an ambiguous role in the Suez crisis and, as an elderly aristocrat, looked (and quite possibly felt) like a relic from a bygone age. Under Winston Churchill, Anthony Eden and Macmillan, successive Tory governments had practised fiscal austerity, minimising public investment and departing from the script only to indulge in 'stop-go' policies to stimulate the economy before elections, creating a cycle of busts and booms that seldom benefited the public at large. Labour also had a talented, centre-left, leader, Hugh Gaitskell who, although he had unexpectedly failed to win the 1959 election, struck many voters as having more energy and vision than the worn-out Tories.

Then again, Labour had been firm favourites in 1959. That poll came only three years after Eden's government had conspired with Israel and France to invade Egypt before being forced to kow-tow, in the most humiliating fashion, to the Eisenhower administration.

THE 1964 ELECTION

The Suez Canal disaster marked the beginning of the end of the British empire. Things weren't much better at home: the balance of payments, then seen as the main economic indicator, was in serious deficit and the nation's infrastructure – roads. trains, schools and hospitals – was underfunded, dilapidated and antiquated.

Yet by the summer of 1957, Macmillan could credibly tell a Tory rally that "Most of our people have never had it so good". Food rationing, a legacy of the Second World War, which had continued in part under Labour, had been finally scrapped in 1954, nine years after the war. Popular culture was booming, driven partly by television (eager to watch the coronation of Queen Elizabeth II in 1953, Britons had purchased – or rented – more than two million TV sets in three years). In the north, manufacturing industries, while in decline, still employed millions of workers in heavily unionised companies and nationalised enterprises. And the centrist political and economic consensus of the era, known as Butskellism (after deputy Tory leader R A Butler and Labour leader Gaitskell) meant there were few clear policy differences between the two main parties.

Despite being ably led by Gaitskell, Chancellor of the Exchequer under Clement Attlee, Labour didn't sweep to victory in 1959 – it actually lost seats and votes. This unexpected setback was partly blamed on Anthony Wedgwood Benn, a bright young politician who, after a brief stint as a BBC radio producer, had masterminded and presented the party's election broadcasts which had clearly failed to resonate with voters.

In 1963, the year before the next election, the whole political scene changed dramatically: Hugh Gaitskell died. It was suspected originally that he was assassinated by the KGB, a not unknown occurrence (or indeed now, although the Soviet Union has long since departed). He actually died from a little known disease. In May, when I was due to become the party's broadcasting officer, it was still adjusting to Gaitskell's death. In the leadership election by Labour MPs in February, Harold Wilson, the shadow Foreign Secretary, had been the left's standard bearer. He had served as President of the Board of Trade in Attlee's government before quitting (along with Aneurin Bevan) in 1951 in protest against Chancellor Gaitskell's budget which imposed token charges for NHS prescriptions to pay for increased military spending.

Wilson's track record meant, inevitably, that he was distrusted by the centre-left Campaign for Democratic Socialism, led by Bill Rodgers (who later co-founded the breakaway Social Democrats). The CDS's favoured candidates were Labour's deputy – and then acting – leader, George Brown, a temperamental alcoholic, and the uncharismatic shadow Chancellor Jim Callaghan. On the second ballot, most Callaghan supporters, alarmed by Brown's erratic behaviour, swung to Wilson, who won with a small majority. When I took on my new role, relationships between the three candidates were still fiery.

The 1964 general election campaign was set to be the first in which television played the most prominent role in communicating with the electorate. Instead of being a kind of assistant to John Harris, director of publicity, with additional broadcasting responsibilities, I found myself briefing party leaders and accompanying them to the television and radio studios, negotiating with the BBC and television companies on the programmes, planning party political broadcasts before the campaign began and the crucial party election broadcasts themselves.

Although not greatly interested in broadcasting, Harris had established an advisory group of trendy young advertising executives to help us use modern marketing techniques. (I never met them formally.) On top of it all sat the campaign committee, chaired by either Wilson or Alice Bacon, party chair, which I usually attended, but which, alas, lacked a coherent view of how the election should be fought on TV. There was also a token broadcasting sub-committee of senior MPs of the campaign committee, which seems never to have met and was, I assume, primarily designed to reassure Labour's leading parliamentarians that things were under control.

In his diaries, Benn says that, before my arrival, he was about to present a paper on the election broadcasts to the National Executive Committee's broadcasting advisory committee, an open challenge. If he did, I never saw it. In spite of this profusion – and confusion – of authority, the party's research departments had thankfully developed clear, well-prepared, well-presented, centre-left policies which gave a firm direction on programme content.

Ultimately, Labour gained 59 seats and had the largest share, but if 900 votes had gone the other way in eight seats the Tories would have retained power. After three losses in a row, it broke the party's election gremlin. Labour entered government, albeit with a slender majority of four seats.

Chapter 5:
Labour HQ

THE PHONE CALL from Denis Healey came completely out of the blue. He had done several radio broadcasts for me at the BBC, and we had got on well, but this time he rang me at home. I was even more surprised when he made me an offer I couldn't refuse – would I like to join the Labour party staff as broadcasting officer in the run up to the next general election (which had to be held by October 1964)? The role would involve looking after Labour's TV and radio appearances, including regular programmes and party political broadcasts.

This felt like the opportunity of a lifetime. I wanted to do political television, I wanted to make my mark with Labour and knew that television would be absolutely central to the election's outcome. It hadn't taken me long to become mildly disenchanted at the BBC, rather prematurely. As a trainee fresh from two years in America, I had been sent to Bush House, the overseas radio service. It was fun but hardly the glamorous, exciting, high-achieving assignment I had envisaged. The recruiters tried to persuade you to become a studio manager rather than a producer. The idea was to teach you all you needed to know about radio technique. My dissatisfaction crystallised when a matronly elocutionist tried to teach me to say my Rs, an effort, I recognise in hindsight, to overcome this 'defect' so I could take on a more prominent presenter role. (The *New Statesman* ran a diary item a year or two later, saying how strange it was that so many Labour figures, Woy Jenkins, Tony Cwosland and Cwive Bwadley could not pronounce their Rs.

I was so upset it took me some time to realise that I had been included in rather exalted company.)

Actually, I under-estimated the BBC's attitude towards trainees. The North American service at Bush House was something of a nursery for talent, with a tyrannical head, George Steedman, and sympathetic deputy head, Christopher Bell, renowned for their prowess as trainers. I had put myself forward for the soon-to-be-launched BBC2, but in typical BBC fashion, heard nothing for yonks – I later learned that I had indeed been selected. Yet, at the time, it was politics that excited me. Happily, my BBC superiors understood and didn't seem to hold it against me. What I didn't fully appreciate was that this decision would label me as politically partial, in BBC terms, ever thereafter.

Labour's interviewing process hardly existed. I met John Harris, director of communications – later Lord Harris of Greenwich and a prominent supporter of the Social Demo- crats – who would be my line manager. As Gaitskell died while I was still at the BBC, Harold Wilson inherited me. I suspect he really wanted to manage his own broadcasting, rather than take advice from a young Transport House official, but happily we soon developed a rapport.

My arrival at Transport House – the Labour Party was a tenant of the Transport and General Workers Union in its grand but fly-blown offices in Smith Square – was just as low key. Over the years, I have learned that you are never expected when you turn up for a new job. It was as if the bureaucra- cy had decided to take the bumptious new arrival down a peg or two. Harris met me briefly, told me where my office was and left me to get on with it. I wasn't exactly sure what 'it' was, having been given no lengthy brief or job description. Labour's general secretary Len Williams didn't ask to meet me, largely because, I discovered, he opposed the broadcasting of politics on principle. Happily, his PA, Barbara Hosking, really did his work for him and became a lifelong friend.

The office was down a remote corridor (but with a good view) leading to a makeshift TV studio, with one amateur TV camera and an editing suite. This struck me as rather pointless because every broadcast I was involved with would be supported by a full team of trained BBC or ITV technicians. Doreen Stainforth was already in place as my assistant. I suspect my arrival had deprived her of the post. I didn't know, until sometime after, that Doreen was in a relationship with – and would indeed marry – Percy Clarke, the hard-bitten journalist who was Harris's deputy. Percy looked after newspaper mechanics, not ideas, a necessary cog in any successful party machine.

The members of Labour's headquarters staff belonged to one of two tribes. There were the political workhorses, long-serving men who had risen through the ranks of constituency party agents (and one woman, Sarah Barker, the party's successful national agent) or, like Len Williams, learned their trade in the unions. The other tribe consisted of bright young men and women, recent economics and politics graduates on the first step to the House of Commons who, because they were constantly searching for a winnable seat, never stayed long. They had two good bosses, Peter Shore and David Ennals. Peter masterminded domestic policy and the election manifesto, while David looked after foreign policy. Somehow broadcasting didn't fit into either tribe, although the research departments provided essential, pertinent briefings for programmes.

Some years later, I learned of the shenanigans that had led

to my appointment. For the 1959 election, the party's broadcasting had been orchestrated by the very model of a bright young man, Tony Benn (Anthony Wedgwood Benn as he was then). Good-looking, ambitious and well off, of good Labour stock, with a lovely American wife, he had a modicum of broadcasting experience (actually, exactly the same as mine, right down to the same desk at the BBC's Bush House). He was a Prime Minister-In-Waiting then, not yet a radical firebrand. He had, after much difficulty, given up his father's hereditary peerage to return to the Commons. Labour's bright hope for the future, Tony looked destined to succeed.

As chair of Labour's broadcasting committee, Benn had been given control of the party's 1959 TV election broadcasts. He revamped them radically eschewing straight 'ministerial' talks to camera for a documentary type format, modelled on Cliff Michelmore's popular TV magazine show *Tonight*, with himself as presenter. He did it rather well and, by the standards of political broadcasts, achieved good ratings. There was, though, one rather important thing he got wrong. When Labour unexpectedly lost, post-mortem market research suggested that, as Tony's formula left only a tiny closing slot for Gaitskell to address the nation, he had failed to project the Labour leader as potential Prime Minister and distracted from the party's core policies.

In response, Gaitskell called for the abolition of the party's broadcasting committee, chaired by Benn, so that future programming could be determined by the leader, the parliamentary party's campaign committee and the chief whip. Harold Wilson admired Tony at the time and, after Gaitskell's death, spared the committee the axe but didn't define a new policy. Consequently, Labour's broadcasting policy remained a constant battle. Tony Benn was not giving up. I, Janus-like, was to find a way between two competing schools of thought. As Harris kept his head down, I was on my own. That was the scenario when I turned up, ignorant and innocent, at Transport House on the first of May 1963.

I realise now that I was sold something of a pup. With Tony supposedly side-lined, the party lacked someone to be in charge of broadcasting for the General Election, now certainly no more than 18 months off. Healey and I had got on well, and he recommended me for the staff job. No-one thought to tell me of the problems that led to my appointment, leaving me to cope with an aggrieved Tony Benn.

Chapter 6:

Broadcasting and Harold Wilson

WORKING FOR HAROLD WILSON was a tremendous privilege. He was Leader of the Opposition when I first went to work for the Labour Party as broadcasting officer for the 1964 general election, and we kept in touch until he retired as Prime Minister in 1976. Elected leader after Gaitskell's untimely death, he had only eighteen months to establish himself before the election.

By the time I arrived, I had only some twelve months to plan for the television and radio programmes for the General Election, in which time we also had some five 'routine' television and a number of radio party political broadcasts, plus of course regular TV and radio coverage of the political scene which was hotting up as the date for the election neared – it was actually on just about the last date permitted by law as the Conservatives tried to recover their position from the lows to which it had descended. Dealing with this sort of pressure seems to have been part of my life.

Wilson was often castigated as left-wing and self-seeking, but he was intelligent, pragmatic, approachable, good humoured, blessed with a deep understanding of people. A grammar school boy, as different as possible to his Etonian Tory predecessors. He was no socialist ideologue: his obsession was social justice. He got things done which needed to be done, even when he was sometimes personally unconvinced. He was never happier than when chatting to leading journalists with brandy and cigar – or pipe – to hand. He was one of the great Prime Ministers, hampered by the state of the British economy and the vexing question of whether or not to devalue the pound sterling, which could do immense damage to the party in office (as, indeed, it did).

For some reason, more rumour and gossip swirled around Harold Wilson than around most Prime Ministers. I suspect this was because he was totally approachable. I saw quite a lot of him during those two years, in his office behind the Speaker's Chair in the House of Commons, with him on the way to television and radio studios, and in my own office in Transport House. Many others will have known him better than I did, but I probably had more casual conversations than most, and these continued while he remained in government. And I am constantly being asked whether this or that piece of gossip was true. Of course, I don't actually *know* any more than the next person, but here are my answers.

Did Wilson have an affair with his secretary/PA/political adviser, Marcia Williams, who was made a life peer as Baroness Falkender? Marcia was close to him and privy to virtually everything he did and thought. She was a powerful gatekeeper with clear ideas on what was in his best interest. The damaging idea that they might have slept together is nonsense, fostered by his enemies, but of great interest to the public, who were fond of Wilson. Harold was devoted to his wife Mary (as, indeed, was Marcia) and I never saw or heard anything which might have indicated even a one-off furtive kiss.

Why did Joe Haines, Press Secretary, and Bernard Donoghue, head of the Policy Unit at No 10, dislike and distrust Marcia so much? Both were capable operators, but relative latecomers to the kitchen cabinet, joining in 1974 at a time when Wilson's enthusiasm for government was waning. It is possible that his great mental capacity was already diminishing, something only those closest to him could observe. Marcia had always been ferociously protective, intimidating and repelling 'intruders', a tendency that became more pronounced the longer she and Harold worked together. I bore the brunt of this myself at first but we liked each other and I believe she was instrumental in inviting me, ultimately unsuccessfully, to join the No10 political staff as Labour's troubles mounted. I could stand up to her politely and was able to have my say. It's easy to see why Wilson's new advisers regarded her as overstepping the mark in obstructing their access to him. The atmosphere inside No 10 became toxic but two such well-qualified advisers should have tried to reduce the tension.

Although I am hardly impartial, I'm not sure that the appointment of Gerald Kaufman, in the role I had originally been offered at No 10, helped much. Serving from 1967 to 1970, he never seemed the right man to manage recalcitrant Labour MPs. I saw him as bumptious and egotistical. Enough said. Kaufman as an MP himself was chair of the House of Commons Select Committee on Culture, which called the Publishers Association for a session on the Net Book Agreement (see Chapter 4). Inevitably we clashed. Returning to government in 1974, Wilson appointed him as a junior minister in the Department of Environment, and Callaghan moved him to the Department of Industry. To give him his due, he wrote a splendidly amusing book *How to be a Minister*, which proved helpful to aspiring ministers troubled by their lack of influence on government. He served long enough as an MP to become Father of the House.

Then, was there a secret plot to assassinate Marcia? No. There is such a thing as black humour.

Was there an MI5 plot against Wilson? Yes, but it depends on what you mean by plot. MI5, charged with protecting the nation's security, is intrinsically suspicious of anyone with left-wing leanings, and Wilson was Prime Minister at a time when the Soviet Union was a skilful, much feared (and theoretically left-wing) enemy. Many Labour Cabinet ministers discovered, on appointment, that MI5 had capacious files on them. Wilson would have interested the intelligence agencies for two reasons. They regarded him as an ardent, outright left-winger (which he was not). And, as President of the Board of Trade and, later, a business consultant, he had visited Russia often. No doubt he scrutinised the regime and aimed to meet people in government but, if you wanted to educate yourself as a potential Prime Minister, this was hardly suspicious.

Peter Wright, in his book *Spycatcher*, capitalised on the idea that Wilson was a Soviet stooge because it dovetailed with his bitter worldview, gave him the oxygen of publicity and made him a millionaire. Margaret Thatcher tried to prevent his book being published, sending Cabinet Secretary Robert Armstrong to Australia to seek an injunction there (the case in which the famous phrase 'economical with the truth' became a euphemism for lying). I very much doubt whether anyone senior at MI5 seriously considered getting rid of Wilson although the service kept an eye on him. There were some, at Peter Wright's level, who plotted to discredit and oust him, in tandem with a motley crew of retired army officers, rogue security agents and right-wing malcontents. If all this scheming made Wilson paranoid, who can blame him? After all, IPC chairman Cecil King *had* tried to orchestrate a coup against him back in 1968, a bizarre episode I discuss in Act 3.

My first day at Transport House in 1963 gave me a taste of my new job. Within hours of finding my desk, Marcia phoned me to say that Harold had heard that his leadership rival, shadow Chancellor Jim Callaghan, was to appear on *Panorama* that evening. Nobody had consulted him about this and he wanted to be on the programme himself. Would I fix this?

It was not, I thought, an unreasonable request. Newly installed as Leader of Labour and the Opposition, Wilson would hardly welcome his erstwhile opponent setting out the party's new, post-Gaitskell, economic vision. As Callaghan was still smarting from his desultory showing in the leadership election, inviting him to withdraw was asking for trouble.

I phoned Paul Fox, editor of *Panorama*, instead. He replied that he'd be delighted to have Wilson on the programme but I would have to break it to Callaghan. Unsurprisingly, the shadow Chancellor took umbrage. In Tony Benn's published diaries, the episode is written up as though – which Callaghan instinctively assumed – I had done this off my own bat to prove I was now in charge. How he thought I'd have the temerity on my first day I can't imagine. Thereafter, he and I never got on well, not even when he became Prime Minister. And my impossible relationship with Benn bedevilled my time at Transport House. To give him his due, Tony did come to speak for me when I was the (unsuccessful) Labour candidate in a by-election in the safe Tory seat of South Kensington in 1968.

And so, on my very first evening in the new job, I found myself accompanying Wilson to the BBC studios at Lime Grove. This time my greeting from Grace Wyndham Goldie, the formidable head of BBC Television Current Affairs, was, if not quite as equals, very different though she did express her surprise at my appointment and my decision not to become part of the new BBC2. Apart from a tendency to treat me as a member of her staff, I always found her supportive and a knowledgeable critic. (I returned to *Panorama* at the end of my term at Labour for a brief period on contract). Accompanying Wilson and other leading shadow cabinet members to the studios, on an almost daily basis, became one of my main tasks.

Benn's election broadcasts in 1959 were considered, in hindsight, good television but bad politics. Labour's heavy hitters did not want to repeat that mistake. Tony had fought a long, unsuccessful, campaign to persuade the leadership to define a broadcasting strategy for the 1964 campaign. Traditionalists insisted that the autocued, stylised, straight-to-camera ministerial talk worked best – something they saw as a sign of political machismo – but others, like Benn, argued that Labour should use television to present a more modern image.

I suspect that Healey had recommended me to Gaitskell as a young broadcaster who could devise a format that highlighted the leadership and presented Labour as more up-to-date without provoking personality clashes. That was certainly what I tried to do. Anyway, as I soon discovered, voters were much more interested in regular political programmes like *Panorama*, *Gallery* and *This Week*, and took party political broadcasts with a pinch of salt – or boredom.

In 1963, as chairman of Labour's National Executive Committee's Broadcasting Advisory Committee (of which I was to be secretary), Benn made it absolutely clear that he intended to take charge of the party political broadcasts. Whenever I proposed an idea for the election programmes, he vetoed discussion, insisting we must remain flexible and decide programme content on the day. My counter-suggestion, that we still needed an agreed format and an available cast of senior people, was ignored. All I could do was get on with it – a necessity that seems to have recurred frequently in my later career. In Benn's diaries, he never discussed the successful programmes we produced in the run-up to the election or how well we used regular programming to get our message across.

His opposition became even more apparent when, in my first few days, I called on him at his house in Holland Park Avenue to discuss our approach. Benn kept me waiting the statutory half-hour (as Robert Maxwell always did), to put me in my place. I entered his basement office to find him, with his legendary pint of tea – not offered to me – on the phone, telling whoever was on the other end of the line that "I am Harold's broadcasting adviser". It soon became clear that, in fact, there was no-one on the other end, and that this message was for me alone.

I certainly didn't believe that, as a new, relatively inexperienced official, it was my place to make the big decisions. Wilson had already made the sort of election programmes he wanted pretty clear. The others, Bert Bowden (the chief whip), Peter Shore (head of home research), David Ennals (head of international research) Shirley Williams, Chris Mayhew, David Kingsley, the advertising guru who headed John Harris's publicity group, and, of course, Marcia Williams, all had their say.

Feeling that Tony had well and truly set out his view of our future relationship I found it difficult to have open discussions with him. A few weeks later, he came into my office, bubbling with his boyish enthusiasm, to announce that he had hired a film crew who had made an acclaimed *cinema verité* about the Algerian civil war, to make magazine inserts for our election broadcasts. This was completely contrary to the concept I had been given, and absorbed much of my not-very-large budget.

The film crew, who ran their own production company, Mithras, were talented, innovative and, although fired up with true socialist enthusiasm, less motivated by the humdrum task of political persuasion. I really liked Maurice Hatton, David Naden, John Irving and Joan Hills who were creative and inspired. That said, I wasn't convinced they would deliver the short, powerful magazine items Benn wanted. At our first meeting, having said they needed 45 minutes to do a good job on Vietnam, 30 minutes each on housing and education, etc, they were dismayed when I explained our election slots ranged from five to fifteen minutes.

Our objectives were reasonably clear. First of all, we had to make Wilson as Labour's new leader credible as a potential Prime Minister. He had been chosen more because of George Brown's inadequacies than his own talent and vision. Secondly, we needed to promote Labour as a responsible party of change in a moribund society. And we had to rebut Tory charges that Wilson was a one-man-band with no capable senior colleagues. Labour actually had an extraordinarily strong team, apart from Brown and Callaghan, up and coming stars like Denis Healey, Roy Jenkins, Tony Crosland and Shirley Williams. Advised by Labour's research departments, this team was ready to form a capable, progressive, government. My job was to get this message across to voters.

At first sight Wilson did not seem particularly telegenic – in the way that, say John F Kennedy was – but he had mastered the medium, coming across as an able, even ruthless, politician – just what the country needed, many people felt, after 13 years of often calamitous Tory government. The secrets of his success were his relaxed, not at all pompous, style, wit, sanity, and careful but concealed preparation. His famous pipe was an endearing prop, both integral to his carefully cultivated image as a man of the people, and extremely useful because it gave him time to think. It also helped that interviewers liked him.

After an evening broadcast, I would drive Wilson back to his home in Golders Green, where I'd be offered a glass of brandy, or three – drink and drive rules being less strict then – while we planned and gossiped. Once, after a Sunday religious TV programme at Elstree, my car was parked in his short steeply sloping driveway, and he went out onto the street to guide me out. My driving was bumpy, to say the least, and I reversed in fits and starts, so that Harold probably had a narrow escape from becoming yet another Prime-Minister-Who-Never-Was. Fortunately my broadcasting colleague Erskine Childers lived just around the corner, and I never learned how he felt, opening the door late that Sunday evening to a rather-drunk political adviser asking for a bed for the night.

At my first meeting of the National Executive's Broadcasting Committee, I set out to plan Labour's first TV party political broadcast. Each party had a quota of programmes before and during the election campaign. The BBC, which then monopolised the production of these broadcasts, allocated each party an experienced producer, in our case Stanley Hyland, highly regarded by Wilson as his 'gold microphone in waiting'. Hyland threw himself enthusiastically into the task and gave individual TV training to almost every Labour parliamentary candidate, as other BBC producers did for the Conservatives and Liberals

My main contact at the BBC was John Grist, the BBC's head of current affairs television, who became a good friend, and his assistant, Margaret Douglas, proved unfailingly helpful whenever we tried to do something different. In charge of the BBC's election coverage, John edited the principal serious political programme, *Gallery*, and, during the campaign, *Election Forum*, presented by Robin Day.

Relishing their newfound freedom to cover politics, the commercial television companies had packed election schedules, providing better regional coverage than the BBC. Granada covered northern England brilliantly, sharpening its reputation as an innovative broadcaster under Barry Head and David Plowright, who were determined to make the channel a leading player in political TV. Granada's hard hitting *World in Action*, produced by Alex Valentine, was as good as the current affairs programmes on the London channels. Alastair Burnet and Jeremy Isaacs were prime movers in Associated Rediffusion's coverage.

Shirley Williams suggested the idea for Labour's first pre-election party broadcast. The Conservatives, in government for twelve years, had just launched an expensive national billboard campaign, along the lines of *Fifteen New Schools a Week with the Tories*, and other similar slogans. Shirley astutely noticed that these claims were based not on their actual record but on future intent, and suggested we hit back by quoting the real figures over their time in power.

Great idea. We had the billboards photographed, got the party research department on board, and airbrushed out the claims. So, with hardly a politician in sight, but with a commentary dubbed before the broadcast, we could show the misleading poster claims fading into the actual figures. We didn't need to do much more – on that occasion – than give Wilson five minutes at the end to ram the message home. The viewing figures – in those days we were on all channels simultaneously

– were sensational, and the Tories soon took the posters down.

For the next party political broadcast, we wanted to show how the Conservatives deliberately manipulated the economy in the run up to general elections – and after them. Our problem was how to display dull statistics. In those primitive days, they were usually shown on TV with rather clumsy wooden charts, called Wurmsers, made by the splendidly named Alfred Wurmser. That left little scope to show changing trends. I wondered whether we could use two back projectors (Eidophors) with alternating images to create a giant chart showing changes. In front, Christopher Mayhew, Labour MP and former *Panorama* presenter, took viewers through it, pointing to the relevant data – not possible with Wurmsers. As I say, primitive, but it was new and different at the time.

A third idea came to me as I considered how best to use our five election broadcasts to show off Labour's strong team. Limited by time, money and TV technology, we used big photo blow-ups of schools, hospitals and the like behind the relevant shadow minister – thereby introducing several Labour front benchers in one programme.

One borrowed, yet innovative, idea died before it saw the light of day. At the time, there was an eminent series of extended TV interviews presented by John Freeman, *Face to Face*. The title scenes featured drawings of the celebrity guest by the Polish artist, Feliks Topolski, who used a series of strong charcoal lines to create striking facial resemblances. Our programme was to be on the night of the State Opening of Parliament in October 1963, and Herbert Bowden, Chief Whip, wanted us to use it to demolish the Conservative programme set out in the Queen's Speech. The risky George Brown was to present.

I persuaded Topolski to produce a series of drawings of

the State Opening – coaches and Queen and all – which we could use to open the programme, before panning along his charcoal portraits of the Labour front bench, pausing on the illustration of Brown and then mixing into the real thing. Simple enough, but hopefully attention-grabbing. The BBC didn't object to this blatant theft of the *Face to Face* format and Labour's leaders trooped along one by one to Topolski's studio in the arches at Waterloo Station where a marvellous series of portraits was produced.

A day or two before the broadcast, I was summoned to Harold Wilson's office in the House of Commons, where I found an agitated Benn insisting that Topolski's drawings showed the Labour leader in an unfavourable light and must be withdrawn. Why, he wondered, couldn't we use the (bland) portrait of Wilson that had recently featured on the cover of *Time* magazine?

Topolski's portrait was frank – showing the Leader of the Opposition rather stern and unsmiling on the front bench – but also a first class likeness. Benn prevailed, leaving me to break the news to the artist. The portraits did ultimately see the light of day – Topolski gave them to the *Sunday Times* which published them in its colour magazine, ironically providing good publicity for a future Labour government.

The 'photo-blow-ups' programme established the prototype for our planned election broadcasts. We expanded the idea into a large parabolic screen mounted with blow-up pictures in front of which our chosen speakers could address the nation. This allowed us to make the programmes more flexible, with long shots, tracking, close-ups and background. In a corner of the studio was the formal 'Downing Street set' from where Wilson had five minutes to reinforce the key points. (The final programme, three days before polling day, would be devoted to Wilson.) The BBC's top designer produced a model of the proposed set and Johnny Dankworth agreed to write title music. The idea met with general approval and all seemed set for a series of persuasive programmes.

As election day loomed, I spent hours planning the programmes with Stanley Hyland. When I asked him how our new set was going, he told me that he had been to see it, it was just the job but I couldn't inspect it because it had been dismantled and was in storage.

We arrived in the studio in the Television Centre on the day of our first TV election broadcast. There was our screen and there was the Downing Street set in the corner. I asked for the studio lights to be turned on, keen to see how our innovative idea had worked out. I was appalled. Instead of the photo blow-ups, the designer had painted an abstract design in bright colours, with jazzy cut-outs in the screens so that lights could show through from the rear.

Up in the studio gallery, we debated what to do. I could hardly get a word in edgeways. Inevitably, for that programme at least, we had to fall back on the straight talking heads format. Wilson was happy. In truth, this was what he liked.

Looking back more than 55 years later, I find it hard to believe that the disaster was not a set up. The instructions to the BBC were precise and could hardly have been that badly misunderstood. Stanley Hyland, the BBC's director for the programmes, had worked with Tony Benn over the years, knew he was chairman of Labour's – but not the campaign's – broadcasting committee, and would have taken any comments or advice from him seriously. For his part, Benn felt aggrieved that the election broadcasts had been taken off his hands, feeling it was a judgement on his enterprising programmes in 1959.

Like most ambitious politicians, he could be unscrupulous when he wanted. With the set discarded, he may have felt he could present the programmes again. In an extensive interview in 1998, Tony told BBC executive Frank Gillard that he managed Labour's broadcasts through 1964 and only stopped because he was appointed Postmaster General, with some ministerial responsibility for broadcasting. This rewrite of history showed how badly being sidelined still rankled.

Percy Clarke put forward the idea for an effective later programme, a 15-minute outside broadcast from a sitting room in Highgate, with (loyal) voters putting questions to a panel in the studio. Wilson's final broadcast was from Manchester. Ted Willis, writer of the cosy police drama *Dixon of Dock Green*, and I worked on the script at the Adelphi Hotel in Liverpool, near Harold's Huyton constituency, late into the night. We toiled in vain: Harold and Marcia wrote their own speech when they returned from the Huyton Labour Club at about 2.30 am. I suspect Wilson knew what he was going to do with the programmes all along.

The first working class Prime Minister since Ramsay MacDonald had taken office in 1924, Wilson was a northern grammar school boy with a superb academic record at Oxford, who had worked with Beveridge on the report which effectively invented the welfare state. His life story seemed to embody the kind of social mobility that, although overhyped in retrospect, characterised the Swinging Sixties. The second trump card – which we were never able to play effectively – was Labour's remarkably strong list of shadow ministers, many with wartime experience and fine records: Denis Healey, Roy Jenkins, Tony Crosland, Jim Callaghan, Barbara Castle, Shirley Williams,

Ray Gunter, Richard Crossman, Gerald Gardiner, Michael Stewart and Patrick Gordon Walker all perfectly capable of running major government departments. The team of potential junior ministers behind them was just as gifted, youthful, ready for promotion and, in many cases, already known to the public.

The discarded set for the broadcasts was intended to showcase this strength, allowing us to feature nine potential ministers in our five programmes. With hindsight, I'm sorry I wasn't able to fight a little harder. Viewers would have been surprised by cheerful sets and Johnny Dankworth's lively introductory jingles, and watched. And the team would, I believe, have reassured many voters who still distrusted Wilson, and quite possibly achieved a more decisive victory. But it was too much to expect the ultimate decision makers to accept this.

One incident during the campaign caused immense intrigue in the media. A cameraman in the Mithras team asked to see me urgently because he had, he said, been invited to offices in Sloane Street and asked if he could go to Yemen – even then deeply unsettled and strategically important – immediately to film a night-time parachute drop. The offices belonged to a right-wing quasi-military outfit which had employed mercenaries in the Congo. The drop would happen a day or two before the election, and could well, the cameraman suggested, boost public support for a Tory government involved in a military campaign.

It all sounded a bit far-fetched, but I could hardly just ignore the story – "I'm sorry I didn't tell you, Harold, but I didn't think it was very likely." I phoned Healey, Labour's defence spokesman, to brief him. He insisted I tell Wilson.

My first opportunity came that evening, after our turn in

the BBC's *Election Forum* programme, in which Robin Day put viewers' questions to party leaders. After the show, Wilson asked me what I wanted to talk to him about. We paced up and down the studio floor discussing how to handle the story, concerned not to make fools of ourselves but also not to ignore something which was possible, if implausible. Harold decided to write a letter to the Governor of the Bank of England, as an independent authority, to be opened only on his instruction.

Someone leaked the story of our conversation to the press. What had Wilson and his broadcasting aide been discussing at such length? Speculation mounted when it emerged that, after our discussion, Wilson had gone home with Hugh Carleton Greene, the BBC Director-General, to complain, it was assumed, about some bias against Labour. At that time, except for the set debacle, we had no real beef against the BBC. Like the Tories, we kept broadcasters under constant pressure, with country-wide supporters watching for any perceived bias. Iain Macleod, then Tory chairman, asked me in the lift one day how many complaints we'd made to the BBC that week, and looked distinctly chuffed when I told him "Six, I think". The Tories had made seven.

The *Sunday Times* gave it the full treatment, devoting its Insight Page to the story. Why had the Labour leader gone to see Carleton Greene? The truth was that Wilson, always on top of detail, had noticed that the highly popular *Steptoe and Son* was scheduled for 8.30pm on election night, just before polling stations closed, and at a time when Labour would be anxiously coaxing its more dilatory supporters to vote. That schedule, he reckoned, would benefit the Tories. Rightly or wrongly, Carleton Greene agreed. *Steptoe* was put back until after the polls closed. Given how close the result was, that decision could have swung the election for Labour.

The campaign was possibly the last general election to feature major speeches around the country, in the tradition established decades before by William Gladstone. Wilson gave five major speeches ahead of the election – in Manchester, Birmingham, Glasgow, Cardiff and London – which reached a wider audience when Penguin published them in paperback.

Election night was a cliff-hanger. On Thursday night, as the votes were being counted, it could have gone either way. It's been suggested that if Nikita Khrushchev had been ousted as Soviet leader a day earlier, we might have lost. On Friday Labour clawed back a narrow lead. Wilson was summoned to Buckingham Palace at about 4pm. We waved him off. As I closed the car door, I congratulated him and asked if we might see him in Downing Street later on. In response, he told us not to be disappointed if we didn't join him. He now had to work with his civil servants. A couple of years later, I was invited to join the Downing Street team, but that's another story.

A final judgement about the campaign was that, although political television was maturing, we were all – broadcasters, politicians and officials – experimenting to discover exactly what worked and what didn't. We didn't come close to fulfilling all of our ambitions.

The narrow margin of victory was actually something of a vindication for Alec Douglas-Home, who had defied all expectations by whittling away Labour's long-held lead in the opinion polls, promoting, what he claimed was a settled and growing economy.

Party conference: Scarborough 1963
Believe it or not, the television coverage of the last-before-the-

election party conference in Scarborough in October 1963 had drawn big audiences – which gave grounds for optimism. We hoped that, with an election looming, the active party members, inevitably prone to more extreme views, would cooperate. Nightly current affairs programmes on TV, with leading commentators weighing in, made the conference the perfect opportunity to establish Wilson, still relatively green as leader, as Prime Minister-in-Waiting. Before we even set out for Scarborough, Len Williams, Labour's General Secretary, instructed me that television must not interfere with the conference in any circumstances. Had we taken any notice, we'd have lost a golden opportunity.

For a pre-conference BBC report on Sunday night, the elderly Clement Attlee had been lined up to give his blessing to Wilson, the new leader (I always wonder how he felt about this, Harold having resigned from his government). Before the programme, there was a great rally for delegates, with Wilson, Willy Brandt, the new leader of Germany's Social Democrats, and Lee Kuan Yew, founding prime minister of Singapore, as principal speakers. My job was to whisk Wilson out at about 9.45 pm, head to the Royal Hotel to collect Lord Attlee, and deliver them to the BBC's temporary studio in Scarborough's St Nicholas Hotel to go on air at 10pm.

Opening the rally, Wilson kept to time, but there was no stopping Brandt or Lee. At about 9.40pm, I gestured to Harold from the wings. He shrugged back – he could hardly walk off the platform with Lee in full flood. Anxiously I persuaded the police inspector in charge of security to have his car standing by, blue light flashing, siren at full volume. It was almost 9.50pm before I could get hold of Wilson, push him into my Anglia, shoot up the hill to the Royal Hotel escorted by the police, dash in, grab Attlee, push him into the car with his wife Lady Attlee climbing into the back, and set off, arriving at the studio just in time to go straight on set.

I considered this something of a triumph, but next morning Marcia Williams, Wilson's PA, with whom I generally – possibly uniquely – had good relations, stormed up to me at breakfast to upbraid me for rudely leaving Mary Wilson (about whom she was always particularly sensitive) stranded on the pavement.

On the conference's final day – when the traditional party anthem the 'Red Flag' was sung – a public reconciliation of Wilson and Brown had been arranged. The cameras were forewarned about a great hands-grasped-aloft ceremony after the singing and ITN was standing by to interview them immediately afterwards.

When I checked the arrangements in the temporary studio, I found they were to sit close, side by side, on two identical chairs, positioning them as equals. I wanted them separated, with Wilson clearly the leader. ITN's Brian Wenham had no truck with such amateur interference and flatly refused to move the chairs. Fortunately, producer Laurie Thomson intervened: participants in programmes should have some say in how and where they sat. Wenham got his revenge sweet – and served hot. That evening, the *Evening Standard*, unusually on sale in Scarborough, ran a screaming front-page headline and a mock-up of the set I had protested against, quoting my immortal words: "Tweedledum and Tweedledee."

I never met Harold Macmillan, Prime Minister when I worked at Transport House, but I did meet his unlikely successor, Alec Douglas-Home. Indeed, I was sitting with Harold in the Leader of the Opposition's office in the Commons when the news broke that Douglas-Home had emerged from the Conservative party's obscure selection process. Harold famously joked that he was "the fourteenth Earl of Home". Douglas-Home came back with: "But isn't he the fourteenth Mr Wilson?" Indeed, for an aristocrat tarred as an appeaser (he had served as parliamentary private secretary to Neville Chamberlain at the time of Munich), Douglas-Home was remarkably well-liked by the public, and almost won the election, in spite of his obvious unease on television. He once asked a make-up artist if she could make him look better on screen and was taken aback when he was told, "No, because you have a head like a skull". When he protested that everybody did, her reply was a short, unequivocal "No". His performance as Tory leader proved, once again, that what works on television does not always work in politics.

The new government soon faced a crisis over the balance of payments, then seen as the defining indicator of economic strength. The stop-go policies pursued by the Tories – and Chancellor Reginald Maudling – had created a damaging trade deficit (albeit fairly modest by later standards). The incoming Labour government had to decide whether to devalue the pound to encourage exports and restrain imports. Wilson and Callaghan, the new Chancellor, were reluctant, fearing a backlash from business. Instead, they pursued a policy of economic restraint, which immediately conflicted with the intended National Plan, led by George Brown's brand-new Department of Economic Affairs (the inspiration for Margaret Thatcher's favourite sitcom *Yes Minister*). With the Treasury waging a clandestine civil war against the DEA, the crisis dragged on, casting doubt on the government's competence and Harold's reputation as an economic wizard.

One evening, at a Labour gathering in Notting Hill Gate, when the government had, rather desperately, imposed import surcharges to improve the balance of payments, I found myself, in discussion with Marcia Williams, defending these surcharges as an effective emergency measure. A few weeks later, Len Williams called me from Transport House. After immense turbulence, Wilson had decided that he did, after all, need some loyal 'political' staff at Downing Street to promote Labour's agenda. As George Brown had vetoed first choice John Harris, who had opposed him in the leadership election, I was offered the role.

Accepting with alacrity, I was instructed to go on holiday as, from then on, there would be no break before the general election. Marcia Williams promised that, when I got back, the contract would be on my doorstep. As I had only just been promoted at IPC – and keen to protect future job prospects – I suggested that Downing Street should ask the company to release me.

When I got back, there was no sign of the contract. I phoned Marcia, who told me: "Oh, we're so sorry you can't join us." (Her sentiment was echoed by Wilson when we met later.) I was dumbfounded. In my absence, Gerald Kaufman, later an MP and minister, had been appointed. "Come to tea and I'll show you the letter," Marcia said. I dashed over to No10 to be met not by Marcia but Susan Lewis, a junior secretary. I guessed the letter was from Hugh Cudlipp, IPC Newspapers' editorial impresario. He hardly knew me at the time but with Kaufman he had an informant right inside No10. When I got to know him better, he was apologetic. He put me on the short-list to succeed William Connor – Cassandra – as the *Daily Mirror*'s star columnist. It was not a job I would have excelled at but then neither did Connor's successors Clive Jenkins and Woodrow Wyatt.

When the *Statist* closed, in 1967, I had two offers, one to join the *Guardian* as a leader writer. The other, more left field, was to move to IPC's head office as a Group Labour Adviser. That was a watershed decision. The IPC role was daunting as it plunged me into the murky world of Fleet Street labour relations. With my Labour Party background, my new employers might have hoped the print unions would find me more amenable.

By-election

The South Kensington Labour Party, covering the territory from Notting Hill Gate to the Fulham Road, had a cohort of young radically-minded professionals, lawyers, journalists and academics and the constituency meetings were stimulating and fun.

In 1967, before the *Statist* finally closed, I was covering the Labour Party conference at Scarborough, lying complacently in bed and congratulating myself that my schedule as a journalist was much less punitive than it had been three years before, as an adviser, in the same place.

I half listened to the morning news: 'William Roots, Conservative MP for South Kensington, has died. His death necessitates a by-election. His majority in 1966 was 20,000'. I went back to sleep. And woke up. This was South Kensington – where I was the constituency party chairman. I went down to the conference, where Sarah Barker, Labour's national agent, cornered me: "We've got a job for you, Clive." Labour's cause was hopeless, of course: South Ken was truly, madly and deeply Tory and this was the first by-election after the devaluation of the pound. But it was a good opportunity to cut one's teeth for more promising seats in years to come.

My friends Clive and Penny Labovitch provided us with prestigious committee rooms on Tregunter Road, South Kensington. The fact that five cabinet ministers and five junior ministers were instructed to speak for me – and five life-peers chaired my meetings – had less to do with my popularity within the party than the fact that South Ken was only four stops down the District Line from Westminster.

Despite the dismal prospects, it was all exciting. When out street canvassing, I was preceded by a strident left-winger, George Colerick, who put a soapbox down in front of me, whether I liked it or not, to address the throng – even outside Earl's Court Station, of all places. The formal evening meetings in Kensington Town Hall attracted big audiences, most of whom were not there to heckle. It's not outlandish to say that we won the campaign but lost the vote. As we left the count, Bob Mellish, chairman of the London Labour Party, said, "Great, Clive, now we must find you a safe seat." Sadly, that was the last I heard of that.

Laurie Cook, my boss at IPC, was very supportive, giving me time off and helping out with my tabloid-style election brochure which, even by the standards of the genre, included some wildly optimistic statements. My mother and father came to support me in the final days. My Conservative father loved recounting the story of when he was approached by a phalanx of Tory ladies in Barkston Gardens. "Excuse me, sir, can I rely on your support for my husband, Sir Brandon Rhys Williams, your Tory candidate?" My father gravely raised his hat: "Good afternoon, Lady Rhys Williams. Can I rely on your support for my son, Clive Bradley, your Labour candidate?"

It was a constituency tradition that Labour candidates canvas staff at Kensington Palace as a press stunt. I approached one elderly-looking old boy in dirty overalls and wellies. "Excuse me, sir. Can I have your support in the by-election? I'm Clive Bradley, your Labour candidate." "Oh, I don't know, I'm undecided." When I asked for his name, to mark him off the register, he replied "Oh, Lascelles, Alan Lascelles, I don't think I'm on the register." It took me a while to realise that he was the retired Private Secretary to the late King George VI, grooming his horses in the stable yard.

I pursued safer seats in 1970 and 1974, being shortlisted twice: once at Bexley, a Tory seat which had been held by Edward Heath (though, as it was due to be abolished, he moved to Sidcup), and, intriguingly, to the new seat of Upminster, where I had been brought up. In both, I got down to the last two. Bexley chose a local candidate. I had been briefed that proposals for a new London airport at Maplin would go down a storm in Upminster – improved access, more jobs, better transport and all that. At the crucial meeting, I soon realised that this advice was utterly wrong. It was probably just as well. By then, I was deeply immersed in Fleet Street and the idea of spending every weekend in a marginal constituency was unappealing and impractical. The Tories won the seat anyway and have held it ever since.

1972 Industry Group

After the accomplishments – and disasters – of the 1964-1970 Labour governments, a group of radically-minded businessmen decided to use their management experience to help the party and counter the unions' monopolistic influence. One of them, John Gregson, was at the 1973 *Financial Times* petrochemical conference, at which Saudi Arabian minister Sheikh Yamani shocked the audience by talking about the new Arab power over oil supplies – a development that sparked the global oil crisis. Over dinner that night, we decided to warn Harold Wilson, once more Leader of the Opposition, about this toxic threat to our – and the world's – economic stability

Wilson welcomed us and urged us to establish a group to harness the kind of managerial experience that was lacking in the party. This became the 1972 Industry Group. The first chair was Wilfred Brown, founder of Glacier Metal, an entrepreneur with rather utopian ideas about industrial democracy, who later became a life peer and minister for exports. Other participants, apart from Lord Gregson (as he became) were Michael Montague (Lord Montague), Simon Haskel (Lord Haskel, finance director of Gannex, supplier of the Prime Minister's raincoats, run by the notorious Joe – later Baron – Kagan) and PR man Norman James. When Wilfred suffered a stroke, I was elected deputy chairman under the notional chairmanship of Douglas Houghton MP, chosen by Wilson to keep him in the picture. We set up working parties studying different aspects of industrial policy. As a former labour adviser, I specialised in income policy and chaired Saturday conferences in the Charing Cross Hotel which Wilson attended when he could. My involvement with the group didn't last long, however, ending when I joined the SDP, the new hope of the centre-left.

Harold Wilson's retirement

Near the end of 1975, when I was working on the NPA's evidence to the Royal Commission on the Press, Arnold Goodman asked me to dinner at his flat in Portland Place. When the other guests had left, he asked me to stay for a last brandy and told me that he'd learned that Wilson was planning to retire as Prime Minister in the near future. This was quite a shock, and in spite of its source, I couldn't quite believe it: Wilson had won both elections in 1974, and was widely expected to stay on until the next one. Apparently I was one of only five people who were told. I discovered later that Goodman had also shared the story with Dick Leonard at the *Economist* (to which I contributed occasionally.) Like me, the *Economist* was too doubtful to run the story, especially as it came from only one source.

Years later, I asked Goodman whether this had been a deliberate leak. "It was the only time in a long career of leaks," he said, "when I totally failed." When Wilson's retirement was finally announced in March 1976, I could only weep that the scoop had passed me by.

My other regret was that, in this state of disbelief – and remembering the groundless fears about the parachute jump in Yemen in 1964 – I never shared Goodman's news with Denis Healey, who I fervently hoped would succeed Wilson when the time came. Healey had just savagely attacked the Labour left-wing in an acrimonious defence debate in the Commons, losing him any residual support on that flank of the party. As a result, my old adversary Jim Callaghan, who did have a few days' warning, romped home in the contest, depriving us of Denis's leadership. The inevitable outcome was the disastrous winter of discontent, followed, equally inevitably, by Thatcherism. One of my few criticisms of Harold Wilson is that he apparently did not wish to be succeeded by someone as capable as Healey

During the founding years of New Labour, between 1994 and 1997, I was on the sidelines, like most of my political generation. Peter Mandelson, the new communications chief, showed no interest in my experience. I had not been that impressed by Tony Blair when I lobbied him as a shadow trade minister on publishing issues for the Publishers Association. I had to keep these reservations to myself during those years when he could do no wrong. He proved to be a remarkable Prime Minister, but when we met, I could already discern signs of the hubris that led to the Iraq fiasco.

ACT 3
FROM
BROADCASTING
TO PRINT

Interlude:
HUGH CUDLIPP AND
TED PICKERING

TWO EDITORIAL GIANTS bestrode the colossus that was IPC (International Publishing Corporation) in my time there. The first was Hugh Cudlipp, a gritty Welshman who burst into newspapers as an old-fashioned reporter in his teens, formed an alliance with Cecil Harmsworth King, a scion of the great newspaper families Northcliffe and Harmsworth, who was chairman of the *Daily Mirror* and *Sunday Pictorial* (later *Sunday Mirror*), and then of IPC, which he largely created. King appointed Cudlipp chief editor of the *Sunday Pictorial* in 1937. In 1968 Cudlipp had the unfortunate task of firing King as chair of IPC after the press baron had tried to orchestrate a coup against Prime Minister Harold Wilson, summarily taking over the front page of the *Daily Mirror* for a diatribe against Wilson and attempting to persuade Earl Mountbatten, Prince Philip's uncle, to head a government of national unity.

The other giant was Edward Pickering, aka Pick who joined IPC in 1964, when Cudlipp made him co-Editorial Director. A former managing editor of the *Daily Mail*, he was deputy editor (later editor) of the *Daily Express* when proprietor Lord Beaverbrook asked him to teach a young trainee named Rupert Murdoch the basics of journalism, saying: "Take care of him, Pick, you never know where he might turn up." Murdoch never forgot the favour, later appointing his old mentor as one of two independent national directors of Times Newspapers and then Vice-Chairman of the *Times*. In my time, Pick was editorial director of Mirror Group Newspapers, renamed as IPC Newspapers (IPCN), and then its chairman.

As Deputy General Manager of Mirror Group Newspapers, but with relatively little practical newspaper experience, I became a sort of general factotum to IPC's leaders. It was Pick who, back in the Sixties, asked me to write a long feature in the *Statist* about the group's plans to revolutionise national newspaper production, an article which helped make my career. At MGN/IPCN, I was informally Pick's PA, invited to join him for a glass of wine before he went home on Friday evenings to plan the week ahead. This often involved drafting a speech, complete with the necessary jokes, over the weekend. I drafted IPC's annual report, giving me insight into the scale of the business – newspapers, magazines, books, and printing – and was secretary of IPCN board's executive group, which provided much of the thinking behind various policies, problems and initiatives. This brought me closer to Cudlipp, chairman of IPC Newspapers. In contrast to Pick, Cudlipp usually summoned me for early morning meetings, where it was my task to confront, and help finish, a bottle of slightly sparkling Mateus Rose.

In a strange way, my contacts with Cudlipp were friendly but negative. I am pretty certain he offered Gerald Kaufman to Harold

Wilson as his Party Political Secretary at my expense. (In the long run, he might have done me a favour because, although I might have become an MP, the times were against me and being in continuous opposition is not much fun). At IPCN, I opposed Cudlipp on his two greatest mistakes, selling the *Sun* to Murdoch and the costly launch of *Mirror Magazine*. He never held this against me. I was occasionally invited to his cottage on Barnes Common to bring papers and discuss various issues, sometimes with his wife Joan (who, legend had it, had a parrot that liked to shout 'Publish and be damned!') These thoroughly enjoyable occasions were, thankfully, lubricated by coffee not wine.

Cudlipp was pure journalist. And a brilliant one. His greatest achievement was to turn the *Daily Mirror* from a cheap newspaper, originally appealing to women, into an essential read for the working class, dramatically expanding its circulation. He gave readers what they wanted – news, sport, cartoon strips, girls and pithy stories – and so much more, including brilliantly written, punchy and intelligent features such as *MirrorScope* and *Inside Page*. He hated the business of management – one area where I suspect I was particularly useful to him – becoming IPC chairman almost by default and never enjoying his five years at the top.

IPC was beginning to suffer from over-ambition and over-extension. In 1970, it was merged in a reverse takeover, apparently organised by Cudlipp, with Reed Paper, which IPC thought it controlled through a one-third share ownership. The merged companies became Reed International, led by Reed's chairman Don Ryder, a no-nonsense businessman who had little time for newspapers. This was the first step towards the rapid fragmentation of IPC. Another new broom, senior civil servant Alex Jarratt, was brought in to head IPC Newspapers in 1970, becoming chairman of the diminished IPC in 1973. He was immensely capable but never really had the chance to turn the business around, and moved on to a distinguished career in industry.

Sadly, Cudlipp has to share the blame for this decline, although there was something inevitable about the rise and fall of his great Fleet Street adventure. They say all great careers end in failure. He remodelled the struggling Odhams newspaper, the *Sun,* taking it further upmarket than the *Mirror.* It didn't work. He was reluctant to close the title, preferring to find a new owner (as discussed in the next chapter). IPC Newspapers' executive group warned specifically that it should not be Rupert Murdoch, a brash, bright Australian, who was already showing signs of the mega-newspaperman he became. Cudlipp ignored this advice. By 1978, Murdoch's *Sun* was outselling the *Daily Mirror,* once the profitable bedrock of IPC. The *Mirror Magazine* was another blunder. Cudlipp's brainchild suffered from the same problem as his repositioning of the *Sun* – it was pitched where the readers weren't.

By contrast, Pick was a calm operator – it was once said of him that he could "take the drama out of the crossing of the Red Sea" – and a great journalistic technician who just got on with running things. Both were great leaders and, as they say in obituaries, 'much missed today'.

This crucial, contentious and controversial era in Fleet Street's history has inspired many stories and legends. As someone who was there at the time – at a fairly senior level – I must challenge some of the stories which regularly appear in accounts of Fleet Street at the time.

For a start, I find it impossible to envisage IPC Newspapers under Jarratt as the bear pit and drinking den described by media commentator Roy Greenslade, a one-time *Daily Mirror* editor. A calm, reflective man, Jarratt ran a tight ship. Expenses were, indeed, regarded as a valuable supplement to salaries on the editorial floor but this partly reflected the failure to implement a sensible salary structure and limit claims to expenses which had actually been incurred. On my fairly frequent walks through the editorial floor, day and night, it seemed, if not calm – how could it be, it was the boiler room of a great national newspaper? – highly organised. That said, I was somewhat disheartened when I raised the continuing levels of high expenses with Ken Hord, the *Daily Mirror*'s editorial manager. "Oh," he said, "I thought that was the idea."

Greenslade's description of Cecil King as expanding IPC's empire willy-nilly ignores the way the media industry was evolving in the 1960s. Roy Thomson embarked on a similar strategy, with similar objectives. IPC acquired some highly profitable and eminent magazine companies, some valuable book companies and a raft of smaller printing companies which were being heavily rationalised to raise productivity. Under guidance from business consultancy McKinsey, IPC was divided into product divisions, each with its own company structure: newspapers, consumer magazines, business magazines, books, printing and, eventually New Enterprises, to exploit new publishing technologies. I don't think this structure made the group more productive or competitive but that's another story.

Nor do I accept my friend Geoffrey Goodman's assertion that Mirror Group Newspapers' moves into new newspaper technology were initiated under managing director Percy Roberts in the late Seventies. Development director Stafford Beer had embarked on this back in the Sixties but, as with so many technological revolutions, it took years to adapt to – and debug – the new systems. This challenge was made all the more arduous by the print unions' trenchant opposition.

Interlude:
FLEET STREET AS IT WAS

IT'S BEEN FORTY years since I worked in Fleet Street, the home of IPC and the *Daily Mirror*, in which time the structure and ethos of the industry has changed beyond recognition. My account of my time there – principally the late Sixties and early Seventies – focuses more on management policies and production than on editorial.

Fleet Street itself was oddly unsuitable as the epicentre of national newspaper production, with its giant presses fed by massive rolls of paper. Newspapers had actually outgrown it, a manufacturing industry in part of the City of London with narrow streets and even narrower lanes. The national newspaper exodus from Fleet Street, led by Rupert Murdoch moving News International to Wapping, was designed not just to thwart the troublesome print unions but to give publishers that vital commodity, space. Ironically, this departure happened just as new electronic technology and web offset printing changed office needs entirely by making it possible to separate editorial from production.

When I worked there, national newspapers were still clustered around Fleet Street, although few of them were actually on it. Most of the red top *Mirror*'s five million run was edited and printed at its – and IPC's – headquarters at Holborn Circus, with the massive presses reputedly only a few feet away from the Central Line below. The company's weekly offshoot, *Reveille,* and some copies of the *Mirror* were printed in Stamford Street, south of the river, a dangerous place – I was advised to keep away – and reportedly the entrepot for stolen copies of all Sunday newspapers to be distributed illicitly. Odhams titles, now also owned by IPC, the *Sun* (formerly the *Daily Herald*) and the *People*, were produced in Covent Garden. The *People* and

INTERLUDE

Sporting Life moved to Holborn Circus after Murdoch acquired the *Sun* in 1969. The *Daily Express* and *Daily Telegraph* were actually based in Fleet Street itself: the *Express* in the great black glasshouse (with the *Evening Standard* nearby) and the *Telegraph* in a suitably dignified edifice.

Murdoch's *News of the World* (and the *Sun*) operated from Bouverie Street, near the Newspaper Publishers Association. The *Daily Mail* was headquartered in Harmsworth House, also in Bouverie Street, in the former home of the *News Chronicle* where my mother had worked as a reporter for the *Daily News* (as it was known in the Twenties). The *Mail* also occupied Carmelite House on the Embankment. The *Times* had thundered away at its Printing House Square premises near Blackfriars Bridge since it was founded in 1785, but joined Thomson stablemate the *Sunday Times* at Gray's Inn Road in 1974, leaving the tenant newspapers, the *Observer* and the *Guardian,* searching for new premises and presses. The Sunday *Observer* acquired the Printing House Square building and print works in St Andrew's Hill from the *Times,* while the *Guardian* moved to Farringdon Road. The liberal/left-of-centre *Guardian* had moved from Manchester to London in 1964, separating it from the group's main profit-maker, the *Manchester Evening News*. The *Financial Times* was located appropriately nearer the City of London, in Bracken House in Cannon Street.

The national newspapers were also printed elsewhere, primarily in Manchester and Glasgow, where the *Mirror*'s sister title, the *Daily Record,* was based. The *Mirror* had a development plant in Belfast for an Irish edition, ran a journalists' training school at West of England Newspapers in Plymouth, and owned titles in Nigeria and the West Indies (regarded as useful training schools for aspiring managers). Thomson's journalists' training school was based in Cardiff.

Most large cities had morning or evening newspapers,

represented not by the NPA but by the Newspaper Society. Bill Barnetson, chairman of United Newspapers, one of the largest regional groups, exerted a major – and constructive – influence on the entire industry. Bill worked largely from offices just off Fleet Street and was also chairman of Reuters. Like Lord Goodman, he was regarded as a wise counsellor, untrammelled by Fleet Street disagreements, and a good person to take your problems to.

In Fleet Street's heyday, editorial and management kept each other at arm's length. The editor had exclusive charge of the content of the newspaper while management was expected to supervise efficient production. The most successful advertising sales directors enjoyed an exalted status because of the revenue they brought in. Most national newspaper groups had a single owner, the so-called 'press barons', the exception being the gargantuan IPC, although chairman Cecil King certainly regarded himself as the sole proprietor. It was said that no single shareholder in IPC had more than three per cent of the shares until Paul Hamlyn's book publishing company was acquired by IPC, when Hamlyn joined the board and became the largest shareholder.

In my experience, journalists were considerably more circumspect than the hard-drinking hacks mythologised in literature, plays, movies and the media, which is all part of the romance of newspapers. Most journalists were not graduates but had served a compulsory apprenticeship in the provincial press, with training organised by the National Council for the Training of Journalists, a policy the NUJ enforced. This changed as universities expanded: David Astor led the protest at the *Observer*, appointing a young Andrew Stephens direct from university, arguing that, as editor, he had the right to choose who should work and write for him. Under Gordon Newton's editorship, the *Financial Times* recruited bright graduates, trained them and gave them their head, effectively serving as a talent feed for the high end of the industry.

The principal editorial rule was to keep news and opinion strictly apart. For CP Scott, the *Guardian's* legendary editor, the idea that "Comment is free, but facts are sacred" was a guarantor of good journalism. A far cry from today's curious – and often confounding – amalgam of genuine news, and opinions disguised as news.

National newspapers were almost as controversial in the Seventies as they are today. The main source of popular discontent was the perceived difficulty in getting redress for such crimes as invasion of privacy, inaccuracy, distortion and sensationalism, principally committed by the mass market tabloids (called red tops because of the colour of their mastheads). The political left also railed against the Conservative bias shown by most national newspapers, a partisanship only partially ameliorated by the centre-left sympathies of the *Mirror* and *Guardian*.

Over time, most newspapers switched to tabloid format – even the *Times* followed suit in 2004. Today, the only surviving national broadsheets are the *Daily* and *Sunday Telegraph*, *Sunday Times* and *Financial Times*. The *Guardian,* valuing the larger space, persevered with the Berliner size – halfway between the two – for more than a decade before turning tabloid in 2018. Lower newsprint costs bolstered the bottom line but weren't large enough to solve the economic crisis facing many national newspapers. There were two big problems – the reliance on advertising revenue, always volatile in a stop-go economy, rendered even less predictable by fierce competition from commercial TV – and the stranglehold unions exerted over the industry.

Such issues led various governments to appoint no fewer than six public inquiries into the press. Initially, the main concern was political bias, then the industry's economic and labour difficulties and then, with the Leveson inquiry in 2011-12, the irresponsibility and criminality of reporting practices, mainly hacking of private telephones, by some newspapers. The McGregor Royal Commission, appointed by Prime Minister Harold Wilson in 1975, was perceived as being primarily, and unsuccessfully, directed at political imbalance, but the inquiry also considered the industry's economic woes, dysfunctional industrial relations, and public of newspapers' complaints procedures. (This was the Commission for which I was asked to draft the NPA's ill-fated submission).

The public's constant preoccupation throughout all these inquisitions was press misconduct. Successive public inquiries, supplemented by two reports led by David Calcutt QC on privacy, led to the creation of the General Council of the Press in 1953, the Press Council in 1962, the Press Complaints Commission in 1980, and the Independent Press Standards Organisation in 2014. (This has been challenged, so far without success, by the alternative regulator Impress, which operates within a royal charter which seeks to monitor press regulation). The first four operated as self-regulatory bodies, designed to protect the freedom of the press against statutory regulation. IPSO is funded by the industry and has lay members on its managing board and investigatory panels.

Back in 1975, there was absolutely no way that NPA members could forge any kind of consensus on such controversial matters as politically partisan owners and tighter editorial regulation. In consequence, the newspapers proposed (but never presented) evidence to the Royal Commission focused almost entirely on industrial relations. The situation was complicated by the fact that some groups, like IPC, still made generous profits, which were necessary to fund risky investments in the nascent technologies which promised, at some point, to transform the industry's finances. (As always with new technology, stories of failure abounded.)

The print unions were understandably suspicious, convinced, not unreasonably, that technology threatened jobs and, in consequence, their power.

Fleet Street's intricate web of unions created its own conflicts. The main craft union was the National Graphical Association (NGA), representing linotype operators (compositors) who worked on hot metal typesetting machines setting lines of type in lead, paid according to the ancient and complex London piece-rate scale, which specified the going rate for the many different forms – and extent – of typesetting, creating generous earnings calculated by trackers (whose honesty had to be taken on trust). The NGA also included machine minders, skilled tradesmen who ran the gigantic high speed letterpress presses, replating the rollers for new editions, controlling inking and setting up the complex paper webs running through at up to 60,000 revolutions an hour. Joe Wade, the NGA's general secretary, was pleasant enough to deal with but could be ruthless when required.

The other key unions – the National Society of Operative Printers and Assistants (NATSOPA) and the Society of Graphical and Allied Trades (SOGAT) – represented a larger, less skilled, tranche of workers. NATSOPA, led by general secretary Owen O'Brien, had three main sections: the machine branch, who worked on the presses as assistants (run by Owen's brother Teddy, a pleasant rogue); clerical (typically accounts staff, librarians, typists and copytakers), and RIRMA (revisers, ink and roller makers, and associates, including cleaners). SOGAT represented the reel handlers and warehouse staff who packed and labelled bundles off the presses and delivered them to the railway stations, trucks or buses (the NPA organised coaches when trains were on strike). Bill Keys, SOGAT's general secretary, was very much the capo dei capi of Fleet Street. The key staff in the Society of Lithographic Artists, Designers and Engravers (SLADE), a smaller union led by general secretary John Jackson, created the heavy rounded lead plates to fit onto the letterpress rollers. These unions all operated as closed shops, controlling the supply of labour through their branches.

There were other ancillary craft unions: the Electrical Trades Union (ETU) and the Amalgamated Engineering Union (AEU) – which eventually merged. Their members usually preferred a quiet, comfortable and well-paid life, although if either union went on strike, everything stopped. Rupert Murdoch worked with the ETU to get Wapping up and running, in defiance of the print unions.

There was also the National Union of Journalists. It was less strictly organised than the main print unions (who joked that the J stood for Jellyfish) and competed with the Institute of Journalists (IOJ), a rival body for those who wouldn't demean themselves by joining a union. The NUJ tried to create a closed shop by preventing publishers from hiring journalists with no provincial newspaper experience. The pragmatic rationale for the NUJ's policy, once broadly accepted by management, was that such training, conducted outside London, provided Fleet Street with a steady stream of journalists skilled in reporting, interviewing, note-taking, subbing and, just as importantly back then, typing and shorthand. As the provincial press shrank, national newspapers organised their own training, tactfully locating the schools outside London and giving young reporters experience on local papers they owned or were linked to.

In practice, the NUJ's closed shop policy was doomed to fail. It was abhorrent to those who saw themselves as guardians of the freedom of the press. Newspapers had always used freelance writers who, by definition, were not employees. In contrast, the print unions effectively acted as employment agencies. Publishers had accepted this arrangement for decades, even though it gave them little say over which staff they used (unless they had, for example, an unacceptable criminal record), because the supply of suitable labour was guaranteed. The fact that the union would only supply its own members was accepted as par for the course.

Production employees would then be signed up as 'regulars', 'regular casuals', or 'casual casuals', the former working the full week, the regular casuals working regular shifts (maybe on several papers) and the casual casuals filling any vacancies on the night. The size of the production staff on a particular night was governed by the number of pages in the edition. The number of journalists employed was largely at the management's discretion although the NUJ's Father of the Chapel might, for example, influence how many sub-editors were hired.

There were at least ten unions actively negotiating in Fleet Street, and all had chapels (local branches) in every group. There could also be separate chapels for different titles within the same publisher. Each chapel had a Father (or very occasionally Mother) of the Chapel and broader issues were dealt with by the Imperial Father, usually an elected full-time official whose salary was paid by the employer.

The main wage negotiations were conducted by the NPA on the newspaper companies' behalf, a process that often involved strikes and required in-house branches to accept the outcome of national negotiations. (Local chapels would claim add-on payments for perceived additional work) These industry-wide deals, which required arrangements with different unions to be compatible, gradually gave way to house agreements, providing flexibility when negotiating productivity but creating inconsistencies over terms between publishers.

As the cross-industry rejection of national agreements changed the basis of labour relations, managers became responsible for negotiating with unions over pay, seen as the driving force to increasing productivity. As terms diverged, the need to maintain pay differentials between the skilled and the less skilled meant that agreement with one group might upset an existing arrangement with another, causing stoppages over issues that had been previously dealt with nationally. Publishers were never sure how much clout union leaders could – or would – exert over individual chapels which often ignored branch instructions and called unofficial wildcat strikes. It was perfectly logical that companies should decide how their workforce was paid, but it placed a much greater strain on management.

Trying to paint a fair picture of why this state of labour relations nearly ruined national newspapers is hard, especially because new technology was simultaneously rewriting the rules of management. The status quo, built up incrementally over decades of negotiations, was regarded, by many publishers, as an unfortunate but unavoidable fact of life. When newspapers were immensely profitable, there was little incentive to stand up to absurd demands and lose profitable production. And yet, as the Seventies wore on, the status quo became increasingly untenable. With millions of pounds in advertising revenue being lost to commercial television, Fleet Street needed to adopt computerised typesetting, colour printing and other technologies to survive. An unfortunate glut of unofficial, unauthorised, stoppages also undermined readers' reliance on newspapers as their main source of news and comment.

It's probably worth listing the serious problems confronting management, which all formed part of the brief I helped to implement:

- • Massive overmanning, particularly in the production and distribution departments, which drove up costs and encouraged rampant absenteeism. At quieter periods, half the machine room crew might be in the canteen or just not turn up. This was hard to monitor as management encountered considerable hostility when patrolling the press and publishing floors. One way to cause a stoppage – and not be found in breach of agreements – was to sabotage the vulnerable paper webs on the presses, which usually forced a 30-minute stop in production.

• Shadow appearances by casual labour, some of whom worked under false names.

• Even when productivity agreements and lower staffing levels had been negotiated, there were constant claims for additional manpower or overtime to cover absences.

• Frequent unofficial strikes over insignificant matters, causing lost production while other departments had to be paid. Branch and national officials often declined to intervene.

• Resistance to new composing and printing technologies. For some years, NGA compositors insisted on re-inputting all copy generated by journalists.

In a decade when British industrial relations reached an all-time low (the records show that wildcat stoppages peaked in the 1970s) the national newspaper industry, with its creaking business model, powerful unions, and inability to recover lost production – and, therefore, revenue – suffered more than most.

The obvious answer was to establish an industry-wide union to cooperate with employers on new technologies, settle disputes over differentials and make it harder for one small section to bring production to a complete halt. Sadly, this was a pipe dream. Edward Heath's Conservative government had tried to make union agreements with employers legally binding but this came to grief in a notorious action against some dockers in the new National Industrial Relations Court in 1973, and was subsequently repealed by Labour. The only realistic remedy was for publishers to be much more robust in resisting unreasonable claims and stoppages. For this the industry needed the support of a government which understood its difficulties. For good or ill, this did not happen until Margaret Thatcher became Prime Minister in 1979, gradually creating a new legal, economic and political climate that paved the way for Murdoch's move to Wapping in 1986.

Ironically, the decline of national agreements across industry also spelt the decline of newspaper industrial and labour correspondents as a journalistic career, diminishing press coverage of labour disputes and the changing shape of industry, including newspapers, to the detriment of public understanding of change. The impact of new digital technology on society and the rapid decline of newspapers themselves as a result of the digital revolution was only recognised when it had actually happened – a loss in public understanding and knowledge which remains unaddressed.

Chapter 7:

IPC, Statist and Daily Mirror

WHEN I LEFT Labour after the 1964 general election, I went back to the BBC, this time with a contract with *Panorama*, BBC Television's principal current affairs programme. My return to work on the broadcaster's flagship current affairs programme was difficult. My television production experience was slender – and my time with Labour called my impartiality into doubt, at least publicly. I could understand the opposition to someone with strong party ties having a staff position on *Panorama*. In the short term, the quandary was resolved by six months of purdah in the presentation department, which supervised the intervals between programmes, where I could learn BBC television grammar while not expressing any political opinions.

This purdah actually worked out pretty well. The schedule was an 84-hour fortnight, 12-hour day, spread over seven days, with no work to take home and plenty of time to freelance. I was soon taking my turn controlling the presentation gallery, directing the tight-knit slots in the break between programmes, managing unexpected programme breaks, and making occasional trailers. My colleagues were a lively bunch, the overall atmosphere was slightly camp and relaxed – or so it seemed to me after the hothouse of an election campaign. I got to know lots of people around the corporation and ran the presentation gallery for Winston Churchill's funeral, not as important as it sounds as it principally involved taking an outside broadcast feed.

The offer of a job as political editor on the *Statist* gave me a welcome let out. No longer circumscribed by the discipline of BBC balance, I had at least sixteen pages of a serious weekly to fill, writing on a wide range of topics and commissioning contributions from journalists, politicians and academics looking for commissions. The role also gave me scope for freelance work, particularly for the BBC Overseas Services in nearby Bush House.

IPC had acquired the *Statist* as part of a job lot of magazines. It rated itself as the largest publisher in the western world, with vast newspaper, magazine, book publishing and printing interests. The group's flagship titles, the *Daily Mirror* and *Sunday Mirror*, sold in excess of five million copies, way ahead of the principal competition, Beaverbrook's *Daily* and *Sunday Express*. But the writing on the wall was there for those inclined to read it. The over-mighty print unions were causing havoc, independent television was increasing its share of advertising revenue, and the digital revolution, dimly understood except by a few gurus (notably Stafford Beer, IPC's Development Director) threatened Fleet Street's very existence.

The old *Statist* was a revered but run-down weekly mainly appreciated in the City of London. IPC planned to reposition it as a centre-left rival to the *Economist*, partly because there was a market there but also because it was cost-effective, as the *Statist* could draw on IPC's stable of gifted journalists on tabloid newspapers and popular magazines who rarely got the chance to use their expertise by writing longer articles.

IPC Newspapers had taken its popular national newspapers some way upmarket, successfully in the case of the *Daily* and *Sunday Mirror*, less so with the *Daily Herald*, previously owned by the TUC, which Cudlipp reinvented as the *Sun*, an enterprising failure aimed at aspiring technocrat staff which Murdoch turned into something radically different.

IPC's ambitions were simple, bold and hard to achieve – to radically change the culture of its newspapers, and the noxious environment of Fleet Street by ending the jungle warfare with the print unions. The challenge facing IPCN Chairman Hugh Cudlipp and Editorial Director Edward Pickering and IPC's Managing Director Frank Rogers, was to end the vast over-manning and excess payments by persuading older workers to retire voluntarily and create a more rational regime in which new permanent staff could embrace new technology. To that end, a new and generous pension scheme was introduced, together with an equally generous redundancy scheme and productivity agreements which shared savings accrued from reduced manning levels with print union chapels.

To manage this difficult, if not intractable, issue, IPC set up a Group Labour Office under Laurie Cook, a former managing director of Mirror Group Newspapers, which I joined as a Group Labour Adviser. Another central unit, the Management Development Office (MDO) trained management in every division. Advised by McKinsey, the MBO became obsessed by the then trendy idea of 'consensus management'. Dispensing with hierarchies, we spent a lot of time staring at charts with management responsibilities in circles instead of trees.

I suspect my job as political editor had partly been arranged between John Beavan (later Lord Ardwick), political editor of the *Daily Mirror*, and *Panorama* editor Paul Fox. The *Statist* was not ideally placed to be revamped as a trendy leftist weekly. While the title reeked of socialism and central government, editor Paul Bareau was a respected financial journalist, early advocate of monetarist economics (and a brilliant piano and tennis player). The existing staff were, by and large, intelligent Conservatives.

My parallel career as a freelance current affairs broadcaster flourished, largely back at Bush House, appearing in programmes I had previously produced and broadcasting numerous short commentaries after the news. I became a regular panel member for Overseas Services' annual Budget and General Election coverage and regular presenter of the weekly programme, *Business and Industry*. There was an added bonus to these appearances: if you strolled into the BBC Club across the Strand after a broadcast, you were likely to be invited onto other programmes too – once I received fifteen invitations over a weekend to analyse the revaluation of the German deutschmark, which nobody seemed to understand. I'm not entirely sure I did either.

IPC's magazine editor-in-chief (a sort of roving consultancy across the group), Clive Irving, and his graphics adviser, Geoffrey Cannon (who would go on to edit the *Radio Times*) planned a stylish revamp of the *Statist* which sadly proved the magazine's undoing. Market research indicated a considerable increase in sales but not, alas, as much as the magazine's advertising sales department had already claimed. All the investment was in vain. One of many newspaper recessions struck Fleet Street in 1967. Two years after I joined, instead of going head-to-head with the *Economist*, we were invited to Paul Bareau's home and, gathered around his piano, told that our jobs were no more.

Apart from day-to-day coverage of the government's various plans, crises and parliamentary arguments, I notched up some journalistic scoops at the *Statist*. At the suggestion of foreign editor Jock Bruce-Gardyne (a future Tory minister)

I sounded out my contacts, put two and two together and concluded that the Labour government was about to embark on a major policy U-turn by renewing the UK's application to join the European Economic Community. The report was published as a splash leader, under my by-line, a major scoop for me – even if the EEC rejected Wilson's new application. And Pick suggested I write a 5,000 word article on IPC's plans to revolutionise production of its national newspapers, based on Stafford Beer's prescient vision of the digital future, which caused something of a stir in Fleet Street and was republished in *UK Press Gazette*.

With the *Statist* history, I had a choice of jobs: one as a leader writer for the *Guardian* and the other from IPC itself, as a Group Labour Adviser in its new Group Labour Office which, slightly to my own surprise, I accepted.

I had become known to IPC's senior management, especially Pick for whom I later doubled as executive assistant when Deputy General Manager of the *Mirror* titles. I had even hit if off quite well with Cecil King when the senior staff of the *Statist* met him at a decidedly grim lunch in his ninth floor office at 33 Holborn (it led to the sacking of Frank Broadway, then the rather right-wing industrial editor of the *Statist*: "You didn't make much contribution, did you? Who are you?"). A nephew of Lords Northcliffe and Rothermere, King was a tall and extraordinarily aloof man who had used his considerable financial acumen to cobble together the various newspaper, magazine, book and printing companies that formed IPC. At the time, his word was law.

One day towards the end of the *Statist*, Pick told me that the *Mirror* wanted to reinforce the principle of self-regulation of newspapers and ward off incessant – then as now – demands for statutory regulation by proving the Press Council was doing a good job by publishing an authoritative guide to its decisions. Then, as now, I, like most newspaper people, regarded any government or official control of the press as entirely unacceptable – a terminal blow against freedom of opinion and the right to criticise.

Alongside my day job, I worked as a research assistant to Philip Levy, head of the *Mirror's* legal department, analysing and codifying Press Council decisions. For several months, I spent every Thursday and Friday in the vast empty open plan floor of the unoccupied Midland Bank next to 33 Holborn, with my assistant Vicky Johnstone, making a legal analysis of Press Council decisions to establish a core of precedents for acceptable journalism, under headings such a sensationalism, accuracy, fair comment, distortion, privacy, cheque book journalism, and so on.

This approach, mysteriously, rankled Levy. All he wanted was the cases sorted and categorised, without detailed analysis. Maybe he felt that too close a code of conduct drawn from the cases, common law style, would restrict editorial freedom. Despite all my efforts, the resulting book, consisting almost entirely of Levy's plagiaristic restatement of decisions, sank almost without trace. Later, as I dealt with issues of press freedom and statutory regulation, I regretted that my work hadn't been allowed to help make the Press Council more effective and justify self-regulation. The assignment did make me something of an authority on the subject and, at a major conference on press regulation in Windsor Castle's famed library, I put forward the idea of developing a 'Press Council Plus', an independent organisation backed by good research facilities to keep the code of conduct up to date. This became a major issue after the phone hacking scandal and the Leveson Inquiry.

In my new role as a Group Labour Adviser, I worked under the indomitable Laurie Cook. After falling out with Cudlipp when managing director of MGN, he had been given the Group Labour Office as his new fiefdom. The new role was a major departure for me but I was curious to discover whether I could 'walk' as easily as I could 'talk'.

The GLO spearheaded IPC's plans to reform labour relations in newspapers and print. My immediate tasks included drafting and settling policy on redundancy terms for print workers, an essential first step if we were to rationalise work practices, end over-manning in Fleet Street (where, astonishingly, there was no retirement age for production staff) and change the wild west character of industrial relations. The print unions accepted the generous redundancy terms I drafted. The problem was not persuading them to accept terms, it was getting them to accept any redundancies at all.

I suspect that IPC hoped that with my former history of working for the Labour Party, I would prove more acceptable to the unions and have a less confrontational approach than some of the old war horses of newspaper management. I am afraid I was to disappoint. I saw the print unions as adopting an ostrich-like approach to the future. Instead of working to improve productivity, and thereby increase wages and establish better working conditions, their approach was to protect the old working practices when they should have been working with management – in other words, to be obstructive. In partnership with management, on the German post-war model, they could have worked to adopt the promising new technologies, so that newspapers got there before the giant tech companies which were to overwhelm them. That way jobs would have been preserved and the principal resource the tech companies relied on for their databases would not have been frittered away.

The new job also involved acting as a kind of intellectual factotum to IPC's top brass. I became secretary of the IPC Newspapers Board's executive group, which oversaw the projected reform of newspaper production, I handled the publicity for the lunch of the New Enterprises Division and I wrote IPC's annual report, announcing the new group structure and objectives.

Stafford Beer, a computer guru, founder of the British Computer Society and IPC's Development Director, took the lead on NED and the newspaper production project. His vision for the future, spelt out when he joined IPC as development director in 1966 after a spell as a consultant, envisaged digital production and delivery of newspapers through a distributed network of printing plants in local conurbations, an early internet or intranet.

The project foresaw the industry's present model. He proved his point with a pilot scheme at a colour web offset plant in Belfast (chosen because of the intensely local nature of much Northern Irish news), faxing typeset pages from Manchester to which local content could be added. The initial snag was that each page took 28 minutes to fax. (A trial in Glasgow for the *Daily Record* (Scotland) encountered similar problems.) Computer typesetting still involved pasting paper galley proofs onto an inflexible format – it took many years before computers could reliably provide flexible page makeup, with stories typeset by the journalists who wrote them – rather than by linotype operators. This experience enabled me to challenge Kenneth Baker, the Tory technology minister, who lambasted the British newspaper industry for being too slow to adopt new technology. He had, he told me, visited a local paper in Florida which relied entirely on computer typesetting. I pointed out that, with a circulation of 5,000 copies a week, as opposed to the *Daily Mirror's* run of around five million a day, this was a completely different proposition.

To resolve one of the insuperable problems facing us – how to adapt computer typeset copy to the requirements of newspaper formats – IPC contracted RCA Laboratories in Princeton, New Jersey, to research an automated page make up system. Sent to check progress, I had a fascinating time seeing such sharp-end developments as colour xerography and holograms, but when I demanded evidence of progress on our project, they hadn't got much further than producing column proofs which still had to be pasted onto a paper template.

On a later visit I encountered different technical problems. On that occasion I was accompanied by Laurie Cook. IPC did nothing by halves. A private plane was hired to get us from Manhattan to Princeton (which was only 45 minutes or so by bus from the terminal across the road from our hotel) Mind you, we did get a superb view of the Manhattan skyline. The plane landed about 30 minutes from Princeton, and I was told to drive the hired limousine. As I had never encountered power brakes or power steering, we proceeded to our hotel in a series of Formula 1 starts and emergency stops.

Industrial relations in Fleet Street never made it easy for publishers to introduce new technology. The print unions had genuine concerns about the effects of new production methods on manning, but had long used their powers to pursue specious disputes and, at company level, stage wildcat strikes. As publishers were still making healthy profits, they were unwilling to resist excessive demands and lose irrecoverable circulation and advertising revenues.

Robert Maxwell deserves some credit for facing up to the unions as owner of Waterlows at Park Royal, London, which printed the *Radio Times* which, by dint of its topicality, was highly vulnerable to stoppages. Maxwell was tough enough to threaten to stop printing until the unions accepted realistic working practices. Several weeks of production were lost, but printing resumed on his terms. Eddy Shah played his part too. The story of Murdoch's flight to Wapping is well known, although the determination we showed at the *Observer*, with our painstaking slog in the Seventies to reduce manpower, certainly paved the way. In the end, Murdoch had the wherewithal and guts to break out to Wapping. Even he couldn't have done this if the industry, various governments, and the general public, hadn't finally lost patience with the print unions' obduracy The project, based on computer typesetting and page make-up, new communications technology, and web offset colour printing, would shatter Fleet Street's established model of centralised production centres in London, Manchester and Glasgow, with newspapers distributed by train. Instead, we would print national titles at a variety of local web-offset plants, all linked electronically, and available and searchable to consumers on their (still to be wished for) personal screens. The number of plants planned varied between 13 and 65 (the higher figure represented the typical conurbation areas used by retail giants to establish stores for viable markets).

The proposals were welcomed by IPC's senior management. They saw in them a way of competing with television, with all-day newspapers, regularly updated, localised colour editions and, with shorter print runs at each plant, the chance to carry later news from the United States, and attract advertising revenue from local businesses. This would have put IPC way ahead of the game. I became a sort of one-man spokesman for the project, but it was far too radical to appeal to the pragmatists who ran IPC after it merged with Reed International in 1970, under the chairmanship of Don Ryder.

By the time Beer's project became feasible some twenty years later, newspapers and television were both being undermined by new competitors, using communications technology without the constraints imposed by newspaper production or linear programming. At the time, the vision was alluring, but it was an early example of sensible yet naïve management being blindsided by the thrills of Star Wars. When IPC failed to find local publishing partners to share in the venture, the question arose of what to do with the presses and the delivery vans during the day. One bright spark suggested that we use the presses to print paper underwear to be delivered to subscribers in the vans.

The giant computer Stafford was designing was a classic example of over-reach. The machine was intended to handle the entire operations of a commercial company like IPC, not just newspaper content and production. On this issue, he was not only over-ambitious, but strangely out of touch with the rise of personal computers and the advent, decade later, of desk-top publishing. Stubbornly committed to the vast machines that were then used to crunch scientific and financial data, Stafford banned the purchase of small computers within IPC, arguing that they would be a waste of money when his behemoth came on line. Ultimately, executives began defying him and, after his departure, desktop computers appeared on senior desks (although secretaries still did the typing – on

Wang word processors, which pioneered the widespread use of computing in the office).

A flawed visionary, Stafford still initiated some significant breakthroughs by, for example, exploring new methods of publishing through IPC's New Enterprise Division, which developed 'optical discs' – basically CDs and DVDs – as searchable vehicles, principally for scientific publishing. In a related move, although seemingly at the other end of the scale, he masterminded IPC's acquisition of Butterworths, the then old-fashioned but highly profitable legal publisher which owned vast quantities of legal data that only needed a search tool to realise its value. The purchase price – around £8 million – was deemed wildly extravagant at the time but this inspired Reed International's partnership with the new Lexis database model and today Butterworth generates the highest pro-rata profit of any part of what became Reed International (and then RELX, pronounced ReeLex). Beer's idea of a separate division, similar to Maxwell's Pergamon Infoline, the electronic side of its learned journals, meant that digital publishing could develop in competition with the paper product.

Strategic mistakes
The formation of the International Publishing Corporation (or Company) in 1963 seemed a great achievement, bringing together all the companies Mirror Group Newspapers had acquired under Cecil King's leadership. It seemed like an immortal Phoenix, but over the years it dissolved again as its different parts were resold, and now its descendant, or perhaps second-cousin-twice removed, RELX, is the nearest thing to a survivor, an enormous business – as IPC was at one time

– which specialises in online business and professional data, though with a healthy chunk still based on print.

IPC's size led to its downfall. It organised its companies into divisions, each a natural grouping of similar products – newspapers, consumer magazines, business magazines, books, print and new digital enterprises. It seemed logical enough. But companies which had previously been in competition with each other found themselves in the same group. The Thomson Group, by contrast, following a similar expansion, allowed the companies it acquired to remain in competition, avoiding the appendages which dogged large companies. Ironically, IPC's treasured acquisitions reverted, under their new owners, to a preferred competitive framework, more suited to the high risk nature of publishing.

As Deputy General Manager of the *Mirror* newspapers, I was involved in the programme of merging companies and saw, at first hand, the opportunities this reorganisation was designed to achieve and also its problems – especially over-ambition. One of my roles was as secretary of the IPC Newspaper Board's Executive Group when the *Sun*'s future topped our agenda. As the new Odhams' *Sun* had conspicuously failed, the Executive Group was asked to advise on disposal.

Two obvious potential buyers were coded as M1 (Rupert Murdoch) and M2 (Robert Maxwell). The group thought Maxwell was totally unsuitable, hence the 'bouncing Czech' nickname (although he eventually acquired the *Mirror* titles in 1984), but we were equally dubious, for different reasons, about Murdoch, who struck us as a dangerous competitor. Before we could complete our report, Cudlipp rang me to say we should stop work. Murdoch had agreed to take the

Sun off our hands for the bargain price of £750,000, with a further £250,000 due if the paper sold more than a million copies within a year. Cudlipp did not usually make mistakes of that magnitude. With editor Larry Lamb on board, Murdoch exceeded the target figure, taking the *Sun* well down-market to become the *Mirror*'s nemesis.

The other project in which I was marginally involved was the ill-fated *Mirror Magazine*, accompanying the daily on Fridays, inspired by the weekend broadsheets' glossy colour supplements and designed, above all, to attract women readers. Dennis Hackett, a former editor of IPC's glossy, feminist monthly *Nova*, was hired as editor-in-chief, with a young Mike Molloy (later editor of the *Mirror*), as the editor, in practice, reporting directly to Cudlipp. When I circulated my draft minutes of the meeting which approved the go-ahead of the magazine, I rather down-played Dennis's off-beat remarks, casting doubt on the magazine's prospects. He was clearly just back from lunch, and I reckoned that he might regret the tone of his remarks. Instead, he came storming down the corridor accusing me of misrepresenting him. The episode didn't inspire much optimism.

The approved plan was that the magazine should take the daily further upmarket, but I was convinced that the *Mirror* had already gone as far upmarket as readers wanted. Far better to create a popular downmarket magazine, with sport, romance, comic strips, popular cooking, and celebrities, with the ailing weekly *Reveille*, effectively a leftover from the Second World War, easily absorbed into a new, cheap, full colour, gravure publication.

The project was not popular with the IPC Magazine Division, which suspected territorial motives. Legend has it that, to boost the Mirror colour magazine's initial finances, some advertisements booked for the highly profitable women's magazines were transferred to the *Mirror Magazine*. Not a great start with media buyers. I also had to referee conflicts for floor space between the newspapers' well-groomed advertisement sales staff and the denim-ed proto-yuppies on the magazine.

The formation of IPC Newspapers, incorporating the *Mirrors* with Odhams' *People* and *Sporting Life* and moving them from Covent Garden and squeezing them into the Mirror building at 33 Holborn and its satellite office, Orbit House in Fetter Lane (with a new bridge built over the road) caused new ruptures. Both the *Mirror* and the *People* had revered, experienced advertising sales directors who insisted that if they did not win the top job, they would quit, taking lucrative clients with them.

The only answer was to appoint an outsider over both of them. But what would they actually do? The new structure was supposed to reduce, not increase, management, but a personal assistant, a secretary, a chauffeur and, eventually, a whole advertising sales research department, had to be put into place.

My transition from HQ staff member to Mirror DGM was spurred by an invitation to join the *Observer* as director in charge of establishing the new printing arrangements following the termination of its printing contract with Times Newspapers. After being feted at the Waldorf (Astoria) Hotel by, among others, the Sunday newspaper's owner and editor David Astor, I was warned by Hackett, who had worked there, that "Observer management [was] made of cotton wool." So when I was offered promotion at the Mirror, I decided to stay with IPC (A couple of years later, I did accept a second invitation from the *Observer*).

In those days, DGMs were the management dogsbodies of the newspaper business. You could be responsible for weekend production, attend any number of meetings, deal with security issues, catering, executive transport, clerical issues, misbehaviour, production statistics, and all the rest. All this between checking production areas, including the press rooms, day and night.

Although a few journalists at IPC Newspapers had generous salaries – through talent or celebrity – the rank and file were poorly paid, relying on wildly generous expense claims to make ends meet. I worked with Percy Roberts, Mirror Managing Director, to replace this with a house agreement establishing a new graded salary structure, with expenses only paid if they had actually been incurred. I was left to work out how the salary structure should work. To encourage chapel participation, management offered to discuss a claim for a four-day week, on the grounds that four ten-hour days would enable stories to be completed within a longer shift.

The new salary structure was to be a joint enterprise, with teams working on grading particular jobs. It came unstuck when sub-editors and reporters disagreed vehemently about whose services were more important. Neither would accept the logical answer, that both roles were equally valuable. We did, though, agree on a new consultative machinery, which I chaired and where I won my bet that the first item on the agenda would be the quality of the toilet paper in staff loos.

During the 1970 general election campaign, there was a national newspaper strike called, some alleged, because SOGAT's Bill Keys wanted to help Labour by stopping production of newspapers he regarded as pro-Tory. In the middle of all this, I heard that my father had died. As there was no production – and no apparent progress in talks – I left a message with Percy Roberts's office that I was going home to be with my mother. When I got back after the funeral, as the strike was being settled, I was summoned by Roberts, given a mild roasting for my absence and told to oversee the first production run after the strike, the *Sunday Mirror*. The national agreement stipulated that no overtime was to be paid for any initial problems. I was to keep out of the way and deal with any problems from home.

At 10pm, the end of the supper break, I received a call that the FoCs, assembled in the pub across the road (nicknamed the Stab) had sent a message that production would not resume without an hour's overtime As instructed I sent a message back to say that anyone breaking the settlement by not returning to work would be dismissed. Production resumed.

Monday morning I turned up in the office as normal only to be told by my No. 2, that Roberts was furious with me. "Why?", I asked. "Because of that hour's overtime you gave," he replied. I insisted I hadn't given any overtime. 'Well, that's not what the MD is saying. You should go see him at once." Roberts was busy but his secretary promised to call when he had a moment. It never happened. I am sure that it was explained to the NPA that I had panicked because I was young and inexperienced. I never found out who had authorised that overtime.

My other responsibility was to decide which of the many bomb threats – most of which we suspected came from the *Daily Express* rather than the IRA – warranted ordering an evacuation. This was particularly problematic at the Mirror, which had been the victim of an IRA-instigated payroll robbery.

With our security chief, I had to evaluate, within minutes, the credibility of phoned threats. We had some official guidance – such as the early use of catchphrases to identify genuine threats – but otherwise it was largely guesswork. I probably ordered evacuation about ten per cent of the time. It was a lose-lose situation. I could be criticised for losing production if the threat was a hoax but for endangering lives if it did turn out to be genuine.

With the *Mirror* titles, the *People* and *Sporting Life* all shoehorned into the 33 Holborn, I became Controller of Administration for the new division. There was now a serious surfeit of senior managers, so I was not greatly surprised when my boss asked me to go back to IPC headquarters to prepare applications for the new commercial radio stations.

This was fun. It was the first round of bids for the new commercial radio stations, the first competition for BBC radio after Radio Caroline. IPC had bought the name Radio Glasgow for the proposed new Scottish radio station, enlisting notable Glaswegians like comedian Jimmy Logan, children's author Lavinia Derwent, style expert Kitty Lamonte and Sir Donald Liddle, the Provost of Glasgow, on the board. We had also formed a technological partnership with Canadian radio company Selkirk.

I found an assistant experienced in commercial radio and we devised formats, made sample programmes, commissioned market research for advertising sales (then dismissed by the experts as dismal), and drafted extensive applications to the Independent Broadcasting Authority (IBA). We also joined in bids for the London entertainment and news stations (they became Capital and LBC). But the IBA was reluctant to award franchises to the nation's largest newspaper publisher and we had to make do with shares in the successful companies.

That said, I did get an interesting offer myself. Our technical partner in Glasgow, the Canadian broadcaster Selkirk, was part of another consortium applying for the London news station and invited me to become its managing director if they secured the franchise. Unfortunately the banker leading the Selkirk bid had so impressed the IBA that it stipulated the consortium won the franchise on condition that the banker became its managing director. That evening Selkirk had to break the news. The job turned out to be a bed of nails. Responsibility was divided between the *Times* for editorial, Associated Newspapers for advertising sales, and Selkirk for technology, leaving the managing director with the unenviable task of trying to coordinate all three. After about six months, the house of cards collapsed, the company was restructured, and broadcaster George Ffitch came in to run a unified, and ultimately successful, venture.

Interlude
STAFFORD BEER,
THE BIG PROJECT

"A MAN DOES not show his greatness by being at one extremity, but rather by touching both at once." French philosopher Blaise Pascal's observation certainly applied to Stafford Beer, the Development Director of IPC from 1966 to 1970. At one extreme, he was decades ahead of time, effectively designing the industrial model for today's national newspapers. At the other extreme, he was well behind his time, becoming so entranced by his vision of a supercomputing behemoth that would handle every aspect of IPC's business that he overlooked the transformative potential of personal computers and desktop publishing.

There was no doubt that Beer was a genius, with all the gifts and failings that entails. He could inspire and irritate – one of his favourite sayings was: "You accuse me of using big words that you find hard to understand, but you need big words for big ideas – and you should find it hard to understand." He described himself as a cyberneticist, and claimed that cybernetics (the science of communication linked to the working of the human nervous system) was the basis of all useful thought.

I remember walking into his office one day to find him on his knees studying a vast scroll of paper covered with mathematical symbols. When I asked him what it was, he said it was a model of the computer system he was designing for IPC. It looked far beyond the comprehension of even IPC's brightest managers.

Beer and his visions became collateral damage when IPC merged into Reed Paper Group in 1970. Even if that hadn't happened, he was probably too left-field to successfully lead revolutionary change within such a large media group. Like many visionaries, he wasn't always a team player, although, in his own idiosyncratic way, he was a great networker: his friends and correspondents included Edgar Mitchell, the sixth man to walk on the moon; Brian Eno, ambient musical genius and founding member of art rock group Roxy Music and Matthew Coffey, head of personnel in Lyndon B Johnson's White House.

After leaving IPC, Stafford went off to Chile to advise Salvador Allende on economics but was turfed out by the CIA which regarded the short-lived government as virtually Marxist and accused, under him the ensuing right-wing dictatorship, of bankrupting Chile. After advising many other governments, lecturing at Manchester Business School and teaching Management Cybernetics at Swansea University, he retired to Wales, settling down as a lonely hippy in kaftans and a majestic beard, indulging his passion for poetry and painting. He invited me to lunch, which I readily accepted, though sadly he died on 23 August 2002, just before we were due to meet. He was 75. The *Guardian* called him a "subversive showman" in its generous obituary, which was about right.

Interlude:
RUPERT MURDOCH

BEFORE I EVER met Rupert Murdoch, I came across his finance director, Mervyn Riche, a tough, formidable Australian accountant. He had flown over from Sydney to London on the prowl for suitable acquisitions to add to Murdoch's Australian and New York properties.

At IPC, we watched Rupert's skilful acquisition of the *News of the World* in 1969 with some apprehension (although the deal would ultimately bite back at him when the phone hacking scandal broke). We knew he was on the lookout for something else, but it never dawned on us that he had the *Daily Mirror* in his sights. He got there not by buying the paper itself (as Robert Maxwell did much later) but by taking the Sun off IPC's hands for a song. He then rapidly turned his new acquisition into a down-market, right-wing alternative to the *Mirror* which, in accordance with the ethos of the time, had moved slightly too upmarket for its readership. Reader loyalty, it seems, counted for nothing.

Today, Murdoch is seen as something of a villain, an over-powerful media tycoon who is unscrupulous about using his power for his own commercial and political ends. The phone hacking scandal took place on his watch, though whether he knew about it is not known. News International paid its price for that, but hasn't suffered as a result. This is partly due to the fact that Murdoch's newspapers take a populist position on political coverage (less so, I think, the *Times*, which runs diverse, well-written, columns). In response (in spite of the Leveson Inquiry into newspaper phone hacking), right-wing governments are reluctant to interfere with a powerful supporter, capable of being a powerful critic. People were surprised when Murdoch's *Sun* gave prominent support to Tony Blair in 1997. Blair represented incoming power.

As one of the most famous and notorious tycoons of his age, Murdoch has inspired countless legends and fictional doppelgangers, played on film and television by such stars as Anthony Hopkins, Jonathan Pryce and, allegedly, Brian Cox in HBO's acclaimed drama *Succession*. You need to remember him as I remember him, a young, brash, typically anti-Pom, Australian, with no doubts about what he wanted to do with his newly acquired *Sun*, and succeeded. Whatever you think of him, with his achievements in newspapers and television, he is the stuff with which great newspapermen make history. Remember Lord Northcliffe.

The dramas about him are not always accurate either. The portrayal of the media mogul in James Graham's 2017 play *Ink* – although ably acted by Bertie Carvel – struck me as a travesty. It presented Murdoch as the archetypal absentee proprietor, dropping into the office occasionally from his Rolls in an overcoat to reprimand his editor Larry Lamb for various shortcomings, notably the regular appearance of buxom blondes on page three. This was nonsense. Murdoch was a constant presence in the early days, sleeves rolled up, dictating every move at the editor's desk or the composing room. The 'super soar away *Sun*', as it became known, was his creation. A former *Mirror* sub-editor who had closely observed – and learned from – Cudlipp, Lamb was exactly the right man for the job (although I suppose the distorted image of Murdoch in the play *Ink* must have partly come from him.)

I met Murdoch soon after he had acquired the *Sun*, at the *News of the World* offices in Bouverie Street, in an office he shared with joint managing director Paul Hamlyn. Their unlikely alliance didn't last long. Hamlyn had quit as a director of IPC in protest at the merger with Reed Paper. After just 18 months at the *NoW*, Hamlyn set up his second book publishing company, Octopus, which like its Hamlyn predecessor became vastly successful.

They were both remarkable men. True to character, Hamlyn sat at one end of the office, comfortably on a sofa, looking like a gentleman publisher, though he was actually a ruthless operator. (He was one of the first to take advantage of cheaper colour printing in Hong Kong. When there was spare space in a container, he would fill it with dim sum or orchids or T-shirts which would suddenly appear at Marks and Spencer). At the other end, Murdoch was at his desk, dealing briskly with his underlings. Not unlike Robert Maxwell's style, now I come to think of it.

My next involvement with Murdoch came in 1989 when he sought to merge the renowned British publisher William Collins with Harper & Row, an American imprint he had recently acquired. Murdoch sent an emissary to me at the Publishers Association to ascertain whether Collins' managing director Ian Chapman, who opposed the sale, convinced that it would cause the publisher's stable of authors to leave, had enough clout to carry out his threat. I said that he did. In the event, the sale went ahead. Almost from the start, there were rumours that Murdoch would sell HarperCollins, but this has still not happened, though to me it lacks the glamour of back then.

By this point, Murdoch must have been wondering just who this man Bradley was, and another emissary was sent to quiz me in the office of Eddie Bell, the then managing director of HarperCollins. Whatever the test was, I seem to have passed.

My next, and I guess final, meeting was on my one and only supersonic flight. Flying back from New York, I was delighted to be upgraded to Concorde. In the thoroughly grand Concorde lounge, the loudspeakers boomed to ask if a "Mr Murdoch" was there. To my surprise, the man himself strolled up to the information desk. On the plane, I guess neither of us wanted to sit together. He came past me examining his boarding pass, and was just one seat behind me. We didn't talk until we were disembarking, when we realised we were both reading the same book about Bill Clinton's election by 'Anon', an apparently omniscient author who also wrote about Donald Trump.

My mentor at IPC, Sir Edward Pickering (Pick), had also mentored young Murdoch at the *Daily Express*. They forged an enduring and formidable partnership. How did he feel, I often wondered, about the *Sun*'s unexpected dominance of the *Daily Mirror*?

After Murdoch's acquisition of Times Newspapers, Pickering became an independent director of the group and then Vice-Chair. In 1988, when I was struggling to persuade Maxwell to make good on his promised donation of £25,000 for the International Publishers Association Congress in London, 'Pick' rang Murdoch and suggested that I call Maxwell immediately to say that if he didn't pay up, Murdoch would. That was something Maxwell could simply not countenance, and the cheque arrived that very day. But none of the Maxwells turned up at the Festival Hall at the concert they had sponsored.

Chapter 8:

The *Observer*

IN 1973, THE *Observer* made a second bid to hire me from the *Daily Mirror* to be in charge of setting up new production in Times Newspapers' former press rooms, negotiate new manning requirements, and adapt the buildings for the new requirements. This time I accepted. When I arrived, the existing printing contract with Times Newspapers had just twelve months to run.

A liberal Sunday newspaper, edited and effectively owned by the wealthy, remote David Astor, the *Observer* was my political bible, as it had been for many students in the 1950s. At substantial cost to its circulation, it had bravely opposed the Suez invasion (which I had rashly supported over an argumentative breakfast as an undergraduate) and, in my eyes, had called every political issue correctly since. And yet, by the early Seventies, the newspaper was fighting for its life. I suppose I was arrogant enough to think that the paper's two attempts to lure me from IPC proved that I was well placed to handle this monumental challenge.

The managing director, Tristan Jones, made his objections to my appointment clear from the start. I never decided whether this was driven by resentment at having to import someone from elsewhere, disagreement on the board over the newspaper's future, suspicion of my Labour background or just preparing the way for his successor-elect, Roger Harrison.

In 1975, a few months after I left the *Observer*, Bruce Matthews, described as Murdoch's Oliver Cromwell, who was running the *News of the World,* told me that he regarded Jones's vitriolic account of my time there as nonsense. Twenty-one years later, at a dinner at the Garrick Club with all my past Presidents marking my retirement from the (book) Publishers Association, Sir John Brown, publisher of Oxford University Press, asked how I had got on with Jones. When I told him, he said he was not surprised – he had never seen a worse reference in his entire career.

I don't think Jones doubted my ability, he just didn't like my habit – essential in this instance – of making urgent decisions off my own bat (which was probably why Roger Harrison, the Deputy Managing Director and a good friend, had recommended me in the first place). Fortunately, George Bogle, my last boss at IPC, had given me a warmer reference. And the Newspaper Publishers Association would hardly have asked me to write their evidence to the Royal Commission on the Press if I had been as difficult as Jones no doubt suggested. So not a very happy start.

At the time, Fleet Street was on the brink of radical technological change, but the new systems, computerised composing and page formatting and high-speed web offset colour printing, were still in development. We had only a year before. D-Day, so no time to deal with complex technical issues.

The *Observer's* first approach to me was rather grand. Lunch in a private room at the Waldorf with David Astor, Tristan Jones, John Littlejohn and Roger Harrison gave me the impression that if I accepted, I would be hitting the big time in Fleet Street. When they came back to me, a year or so later, with the paper's problems worsening, I decided to bolster my credentials by hosting a lunch of my own.

I booked a table in the upstairs room at Simpsons in the

Strand (where women were permitted), arrived suitably early and told the head waiter to direct my guests to the bar, where I was waiting. After what seemed like a long time, I returned to the restaurant and saw, to my dismay, that the guests were already at the table, looking distinctly impatient. The head waiter apologised profusely, saying he had assumed they were meeting "the other Mr Bradley", apparently from British Gas. To make things more awkward, a double bottle of Scotch had been placed on the table, from which they had been invited to help themselves.

After the first approach, IPC had offered me a more senior job as Deputy General Manager of the *Mirror* newspapers, which morphed into a divisional role as controller of administration for IPC Newspapers before I headed up IPC's applications for the commercial radio franchises. With this completed, the *Observer's* second approach felt like the right opportunity.

Editor and proprietor David Astor was an aloof, shy patrician, hardly familiar with the real world, although his liberal instincts echoed mine. I only met him half a dozen times in my two years. Even though my task was central to the newspaper's survival, I was never invited to a board meeting. Managing Director Jones was a bumbling antique collector, much happier in the Borough Market collecting political figurines than in Fleet Street. He made himself notorious by touring the offices on Christmas Eve to ensure that no-one left before 4pm. His father was Tom Jones, Lloyd George's private secretary, whose last words to Astor – "Look after the boy" – were taken rather literally, with the 'boy' becoming managing director of his newspaper.

Roger Harrison, with whom I worked most closely, was

an experienced newspaper manager, journalist and marketing man. He was able but lacked hard-edged production and industrial relations experience. Finance Director, John Littlejohn was quietly capable, someone I could confide in, but plagued by ill-health, aggravated by the newspaper's financial problems. He looked unhappy and wrung his hands when I was asking him for more financial information.

The Sunday newspaper, which had offices in Queen Victoria Street, across Printing House Square, had been printed under contract by the *Times*. Roy Thomson's decision to switch the *Times* to the *Sunday Times*'s more modern presses in Gray's Inn Road ended the *Observer's* contract at Printing House Square and the *Guardian's* at Gray's Inn Road. Thomson had, rather generously, sold Printing House Square to the *Observer* for a rumoured price well below market value.

The obvious solution was for both centre-left leaning newspapers to establish a joint production company with a seven-day operation at Printing House Square. Years later, I learned why this had never come to fruition. Peter Gibbings, Managing Director of the *Guardian*, had started out as Jones' personal assistant at the *Observer*, and once confided that, as far as he was concerned, there would be no deal as long as his old boss was in charge. The *Guardian* soon settled in Farringdon Road.

To sell the *Observer's* existing office building, the printing works on St Andrew's Hill had to be remodelled to handle the smaller production run. This task needed to be completed after the transfer of the printing operation (and without disrupting it), with editorial and management offices built over the printing works. A (hopefully) substantially reduced workforce had to be transferred from Times Newspapers, with new labour agreements, redundancy compensation and other details sorted for those transferring – and for those who weren't. New production management had to be recruited, inducted and given the appropriate authority – and systems – to do their job.

My first day at the *Observer* gave me a glimpse of the difficulties ahead. A dead day for Sunday newspapers, Monday was a good day to settle in. The significance (to me, at least) of my arrival was undermined by the fact that no-one at reception was expecting me. Later that morning, I was shown to a small office with no furniture and a linoleum floor which I was expected to share with my secretary. When I protested that this arrangement was unworkable, a space was found next door for Jenny Mercer, the gutsy, ambitious young Northern Irish woman who was to be my PA. I sourced my own office furniture, persuading my former assistant at the *Daily Mirror* to have my desk moved across at book price.

It immediately became clear that, no matter how senior my role at IPC, I would be treated as a relatively junior manager at the *Observer*. My main contact with Jones was through his dreaded Tuesday morning staff meetings. You were allowed, briefly, to say what you were up to, but there was absolutely no discussion or recognition of the tumultuous changes ahead. I cannot remember a single meeting with him at which we analysed our predicament in any depth or agreed tactics on how to proceed. When approached by desperate colleagues and subordinates, he would postpone any meeting to 5.30pm and, at 5.40pm announce that he had to catch his train home, so it was up to us to get on with it.

My project plan, recommending that we set up several working parties under different leaders, didn't even warrant a reply – no matter how hard I chased. All I could do was structure the project as I saw fit. The next two years were, it's fair to say, hell on earth. I had to juggle project management, architects, engineers, production management, and, most time consuming of all, union negotiations. We rapidly moved on from the ping pong table, on which managers had moved slips around to represent the linotypes in the composing room. IPC were contracted to supply two consultant engineers, Ken Taylor and Harry Roche, who supervised the reconstruction of the production departments (Harry later became Sir Harry, chair of the Guardian Media Group) and quickly made themselves indispensable.

Architect Eric Guaschi supervised the building reconstruction while our retained architect Peter Bedford laid out the new offices over the printing works. Sadly, Jones vetoed Bedford's – and my – plan to house the editorial library, indispensable for such a newspaper, on the top floor with an exceptional view of St Paul's Cathedral. That space was reserved for senior management, a category which did not, I was informed, include me. I was allocated a small office reflecting my reduced role when the project was completed, and the library was carved out of an open plan area of the new editorial floor.

Our negotiations with Times Newspapers – principally Marmaduke (later Lord) Hussey – were inevitably difficult. There was just one week in which the *Times* would move to Gray's Inn Road and the *Observer* take over its own production (as would the *Guardian* from Gray's Inn Road to Farringdon Road). This transfer was much simpler for the *Times*, moving into a more advanced plant with experienced management intact than for the evicted newspapers, which had inexperienced press room managers. There were disputes about redundancy entitlements especially for press and warehouse staff who were not being taken on by the *Observer*, settled in time in accordance with best practice. I consulted and negotiated with the unions over the move and the reduced manning levels needed to keep the newspaper viable. Those who had worked solely on the *Observer* printing contract and accepted redundancy – many of them well past retirement age – were paid off. We suspected that many chapel members who claimed compensation had not shown up for work on the *Observer* for years. Not an uncommon phenomenon on Fleet Street in the unions' heyday.

I had to negotiate with a daunting array of unions: the NGA, SOGAT, NATSOPA, SLADE, AUEW, ETU and, in more of a token 'equal pain' exercise, the NUJ. This amounted to something like fourteen chapels – house branches – in all. Apart from the NUJ, every union effectively acted as an employment agency, supplying the agreed number of staff for the required newspaper pagination. NATSOPA and SOGAT represented the most workers and thus bore the brunt of the reductions. They also were responsible for most – but not all – of the wild cat stoppages (said to have finally provoked Murdoch's flight to Wapping). SOGAT general secretary Bill Keys was a tough negotiator (he owned a grand house with a swimming pool – relatively rare at the time) and his say-so was vital to our success at the *Observer*.

Our optimistic target was to achieve something like 30 percent cuts in manning levels. We got off to a good start with so many elderly staff choosing redundancy. Such a target could only be met through a rational analysis of economic manpower requirements backed by threats of closure if negotiations failed. There was some goodwill from unions who appreciated the company's problems in taking on its own printing and were anxious to play – and be seen to play – a fundamental role in keeping the newspaper afloat. After countless meetings, we finally negotiated enough savings to get the go-ahead.

NATSOPA's Machine Branch, headed by the amiable Teddy O'Brien, adopted a personal approach to the talks. I always favoured friendly relationships with the unions, while recognising the need to appear strong and determined. Teddy O'Brien, brother of NATSOPA's General Secretary, Owen, obviously shared my view. He suggested dinner at Frederick's, a top Camden eatery. We would meet at my flat in Wimpole Street beforehand. He would book the restaurant and host the meal. He turned up on time, unexpectedly accompanied by an attractive young woman and an attractive young man who, he said, would be helpful during negotiations as members of his committee.

After emptying my flat of gin, we got a cab to Camden. No hospitality was spared. By 2am, we were the only diners left as waiters started putting chairs on tables. When I tried to say goodnight, I was told they could drop me off at home en route to a nightclub, although they hoped that I might join them. I did not have the stamina for that but they then suggested a nightcap at my flat after which either the young woman, or the young man, as I chose, would happily stay with me. Fortunately, I was sober enough to resist temptation. I don't think the topic of manning levels in the machine room was mentioned once.

The other major battle was with SOGAT's warehouse staff. We made slow progress and, even allowing for the usual brinkmanship, it looked as if all our plans would unravel. Shortly before D-day, Jones made a rare intervention: he would handle this and I was not – categorically not – to turn up at the plant on the Saturday we started up under our own steam.

I never learned the details of the settlement but during the next round of negotiations, we discovered that the warehouse chapel strength, mainly so-called 'regular-casuals', remained well above target, and was bulked out by 'casual casuals' who turned up for shifts without any commitment.

It seemed absurd for the only person familiar with the minutiae of negotiations not to be there when the new production run started, so I went in anyway. Predictably enough, everyone was on their best behaviour, determined to prove that we could do it without Times Newspapers.

We probably struck our best deal with the electricians, led by a former Communist union official from Times Newspapers, who had become the very efficient manager of our tiny electrical department. He came to see me before negotiations started to ask how much we were prepared to spend on the department. I gave him an optimistically low figure. He came back a few days later with a proposal, costing exactly that sum, using a small workforce who would divide the pot between them. We accepted, with some qualms as to whether this might leave us with too few staff to handle emergency repairs on the run. (If our elderly machinery went wrong, we could lose two percent of our annual income on a single Saturday night.) We needn't have worried. The deal worked perfectly. No doubt the electricians, working a four-day-week for us, could earn substantial sums elsewhere on Fleet Street on other days.

The terms we negotiated were more expensive than the back of an envelope, blue sky, projections the management had made, but still represented big savings, reluctantly accepted as a first stage in helping to ensure the paper's survival.

The fundamental underlying problem remained. There was no way that a national Sunday broadsheet, selling a few hundred thousand copies, in intense competition with the market leading *Sunday Times* and the *Sunday Telegraph*, could succeed in a nearly-clapped out City printing plant operating on only one night a week – and that a high-cost Saturday – with linotype operators paid lavish piece rates for a four-day-week.

Everything depended on Roger Harrison's success in winning new printing contracts. I wasn't unduly hopeful. Who would willingly pay Fleet Street rates, and endure its arcane labour practices, for what was essentially jobbing work when the general printing industry had such enormous over-capacity?

And so, just a year after the first round of talks, I was told we needed to cut labour costs again – and dramatically. This time around, I insisted that, to be credible, we must open our books to the unions. This was done, possibly for the first – and last – time in the history of national newspapers. Nevertheless, it worked brilliantly – possibly because the unions knew more about our financial situation than I did.

Given Tristan Jones's grudging response to the outcome of our first negotiations, it strikes me as extraordinary that I was kept on to lead the next round and agreed to do so. Still, I felt more in control, partly because I had only the one project to worry about. Production was running smoothly. The building contract was progressing well and was completed soon after I left. (I never sat in – let alone saw – the tiny office designated for me.)

But then I faced a new complication. Convinced that Fleet Street gleefully chronicled the rest of British industry's weaknesses in gruesome detail, while glossing over its own, Astor told me that this round of talks would be filmed by the BBC. From my experience of TV, I could picture the cross-cuts between our first meetings demanding an unequivocal 30 percent reduction with the final compromises. Besides, who would willingly negotiate with TV cameras glaring at them and recording them, with no say over the editing?

When I insisted that we could not conduct such complex negotiations in this manner, we eventually struck a compromise. The BBC would not shoot actual management/union meetings but would make the film by following negotiations from outside. It was a marvellous opportunity for BBC fly-on-the wall producer Elwyn Parry-Jones. Every time I left a meeting, there were the cameras, and behind them, demanding a report, was Elwyn.

I was not supposed to give interviews – that was for Harrison – but I seized my opportunity one Saturday afternoon when I dropped in to see how the run was going. The omnipresent Parry-Jones took his chance. My attempt to present myself as a brilliant negotiator with a determined plan was rather undermined by the garish beach shirt I had donned for an informal afternoon in my office.

Nevertheless, we did have a plan, which Roger Harrison and I took to Lord (Arnold) Goodman, chairman of the NPA and the *Observer*. The strategy was to allot a period of no more than six weeks for negotiations at the end of which, if we hadn't made sufficient progress, we would close the newspaper. Lord Goodman agreed. We were to calculate our manpower targets as accurately and realistically as possible, write to the unions setting out acceptable manning levels and compromise only if a union could demonstrate that our plans were genuinely unfeasible (which they never did). Roger and I then took the plan to Jim Mortimer, head of the government's conciliation service ACAS. A former union general secretary himself, Mortimer assured us that if we had to close the newspaper, ACAS would help us finalise an agreement.

And that's pretty much what happened. After weeks of intense negotiations, we reached the expected impasse and one Saturday night we issued a notice announcing that the *Observer* would close. We lost that night's edition, but by Monday we were sitting with top union officials at ACAS and on Wednesday had a final series of make-or-break meetings at Lord Goodman's offices in Little Essex Street. At midnight we were able to announce we would resume production with 25-30 percent overall fewer staff from two sets of negotiations. It meant a further redundancy bill. The deal did not, by itself, make the newspaper permanently and completely viable but did put it on a much more promising footing.

On that final day of reckoning, NATSOPA's Teddy O'Brien could not resist trying to outflank me. NATSOPA's machine branch didn't come up for talks until about 10pm and, by then, after a long day's brinkmanship, Goodman was visibly tiring. Teddy grinned at me and said that if I had been more flexible in negotiations, it wouldn't have come to this. It was obvious, he argued, that a 30 percent reduction was impossible in such a tightly manned department, but, as previously indicated, he could probably persuade his members to accept cuts of around 20 percent.

When Goodman initially sounded as if he was about to accept this as a final compromise; I intervened: "If, Lord Goodman, we accept Mr O'Brien's demands, then all the other agreements we have reached today will collapse."

Goodman remonstrated – "Mr Bradley, when I am conducting a negotiation, I do not expect to be interrupted" – before suggesting an adjournment. After some argument, he accepted my point, telling O'Brien that it was either the reduction demanded or no newspaper. O'Brien grinned, shrugged his shoulders and fell into line.

The next day, Tristan Jones summoned me – he had not, of course, been present – to rebuke me for inexcusably upsetting our chairman Lord Goodman. My future looked grim. Then Jones's phone rang: it was Goodman, asking for me. He apologised that, tired and stressed, he had reacted as he did, and was grateful I had averted a disastrous concession. I happily passed the phone to a visibly deflated Jones. From then on, Goodman and I became firm friends.

This was really the end of my story at the *Observer*. After the second round of job cuts, the newspaper's future was much more secure. Astor decided to stand down as editor to be replaced by Donald Trelford who, despite some compromises under Tiny Rowland and Lonrho's ownership, largely maintained the paper's editorial integrity and quality.

It also became clear that, with recent crises resolved, the board felt that Jones too had to go. This left two possible successors: Roger or myself. I recognised that Roger had been recruited specifically to succeed and, although I had done what I had been hired to do, he was unlikely to want to work closely with me.

Goodman saved me from disaster, insisting on double the paltry settlement Jones had offered. As NPA chairman, he proposed me to the NPA Council as its director, a motion lost by a single vote. (The successful candidate lasted for only six months, so I was probably spared disaster). He asked me instead to draft the NPA's evidence to the Royal Commission on the Press, and then suggested me to the (book) Publishers Association as chief executive.

I followed the *Observer's* future wanderings from a distance – the acquisition by American oil company, Atlantic Richfield, the sale to Tiny Rowland of Lonrho (who saw particular benefits from owning a newspaper with such strong ties to African governments) and eventually, logic fulfilled, the merger with its political soul mate, the *Guardian.*

The NPA's official history says this of the *Observer* negotiations:

With profits fast disappearing, there was only one way forward – to reduce costs in all areas; and in July 1975 management in addressing the unions called for a 33 per cent reduction in manning levels. There then followed weeks of hard negotiation – including shortfalls with disrupted print runs – until finally a 25 per cent reduction was agreed. This meant the loss of 88 full-time and 160 part-time jobs. Although not all the aims had been achieved, the negotiation had been the most successful by any Fleet Street management.

According to his biographer, Jeremy Lewis, Astor believed that Lord Goodman was the 'real hero of the negotiations, who said only one cross word, and that to a member of our team' [*i.e. me*]. As magnificent as Goodman was that final Wednesday, the detailed slog had already been done, as per the negotiating plan Roger and I had agreed with Arnold and ACAS. The final drama was staged to convince the unions that there was absolutely no further room for manoeuvre. Astor never understood how close Goodman and I had become, as colleagues and friends. He was surprised to see me at Arnold's funeral in the summer of 1995, wearing a yarmulke loaned by Goodman's chauffeur. It says a lot about Astor's personality – and our relationship – that the last time I saw him, we stood, silently, side by side in the urinals at the Reform Club.

Royal Commission on the Press

Harold Wilson set up the Royal Commission on the Press, a high-level public investigation – and the last one to sit before Margaret Thatcher effectively abolished Royal Commissions as tardy and ineffective – because of growing public disquiet about the future of newspapers. There were three main causes for concern: chronically bad labour relations, allegedly inadequate procedures for complaints against editorial abuse, and the dominance of Tory-supporting national newspapers.

Wilson was seriously worried about the bias against Labour. While I was at the *Observer*, he had offered to broker a deal for IPC to manage the left-leaning Sunday paper through a trust similar to the one governing the *Times*, to ensure its survival (in the event, it might not have been as secure a haven as Wilson anticipated). Astor had rejected the idea, partly because he was upset by the government's trade union legislation supporting closed shops, which he feared the National Union of Journalists would exploit. I had to find a way through these thickets, get the approval of the NPA Council, and, ideally, avoid upsetting the print unions too much. My job was to tour Fleet Street, talk to proprietors and senior managers, and try to gather a consensus.

In the event, my work was largely aborted when Marmaduke Hussey, Managing Director of Times Newspapers, burst into the NPA Council convened to agree the draft to announce that on the issue of most concern to the proprietors, poor labour relations, he had talked to SOGAT's Bill Keys who had persuaded him that these matters were best dealt with without government intervention, and on which the unions would be helpful. It was a few years before journalists were allowed to computer typeset their copy, and even then it had to be reset by the NGA's linotype operators, a practice which was only discontinued with Murdoch's move to Wapping.

In spite of the Royal Commission, the most serious disputes on the alleged – and sometimes actual – misbehaviour of national newspaper journalists still rage today, 50 years later. National newspapers' principal response to the Royal Commission was to strengthen the Press Council, reconstituting it as the Press Complaints Commission. This endured until 2014 when public and political outrage over phone hacking led the press to replace it with the Independent Press Standards Organisation.

Editorial ethics was the issue in the Royal Commission's terms of reference of most concern to the general public – and to MPs. Here I had form, having drafted a book analysing Press Council adjudications on readers' complaints about inaccuracy, invasion of privacy, sensationalism, unbalanced political coverage, cheque book journalism and other regular complaints. Critics argued that such transgressions were caused by newspapers' all-consuming drive to sell more copies. My work had shown, at least to my satisfaction, that Press Council rulings were, usually, well-considered and appropriate, but much of that good work was undone by newspapers' reluctance to publish the adjudications prominently enough to convince a sceptical public that the system was working. The furore raised by MPs, who apparently received bagfuls of letters complaining about negative adjudications, seemed overblown to me. Readers who did not like a decision were predisposed to find someone else to complain to. Nor was public indignation to be entirely taken at face value: many of those who deplored the red tops' excesses in vox pops thoroughly enjoyed reading them.

I had proposed, at the aforementioned conference in

Windsor Castle's Royal Library, that, above all, the Press Council needed its own research capability so that it could refine and revise its guidelines to help editors, an option I dubbed 'Press Council Plus'. This carried the day in the debates that followed. In the late Eighties, with the public and many politicians convinced that the tabloids were running amok, the Home Office set up the Calcutt inquiries into the questions of privacy and the press self-regulation. The industry did, as Calcutt recommended, replace the Press Council with a better resourced Press Complaints Commission, but he later described this body as "set up by the industry, dominated by, and operating to a code of practice devised by the industry, which is over-favourable to the industry."

Thirty years later, the PCC was fatally discredited by the phone hacking scandal, which prompted the government to set up another judicial inquiry led, this time, by High Court judge Sir Brian Leveson. Once again, there were calls for statutory regulation, which were hotly debated at CICI with the relevant government ministers (see Act 5). Such drastic measures were avoided, once again as the press gave further guarantees of good behaviour and, in 2014, established the Independent Press Standards Organisation (IPSO) which was said to be stronger than the PCC which, in turn, had reputedly been stronger than the Press Council. A few smaller newspapers and journals opted for regulation by a statutory body under Royal Charter, the Press Regulation Panel, which has authorised Impress as a self-regulatory body, but most national newspapers signed up to IPSO. (The *Guardian* and *Financial Times* run their own complaints procedure.) The Conservative government initially took a proactive line, passing legislation to the effect that publications which did not join the statutory regulatory body would be liable for the costs of defending a libel action even if they won. This extraordinary reversal of the long-established legal principle that the winner should be able to recover their costs was eventually dropped.

The question of political imbalance remains perplexing. There is no doubt that the vast majority of national newspapers were/are pro-Conservative, a bias that has become more entrenched in recent years, shaping news reporting as well as comment. Even though newspapers have lost sales and influence, they can still shape public opinion, in part because they help set the agenda for the media as a whole. Any solution requiring some form of legislative/statutory control would fly straight in the face of press freedom and probably threaten the entire industry. Like any commercial undertaking, newspapers require investment, which has usually been provided by wealthy individuals seeking public and political influence, and they are unlikely to bankroll anodyne newspapers bound by the kind of impartiality rules embedded in the BBC's Royal Charter.

The solution may lie, in part, in the ethical rule of journalism set down by the *Guardian*'s editor C P Scott in the Thirties: "Comment is free, facts are sacred". This may not go far enough for some. Comments derived from factual inaccuracies are as unethical as fabricated stories. Yet Scott's axiom may be the best – or in Churchillian terms, the least-worst – remedy we have. And in the modern digital age the survival of newspapers, privileged in law, is dependent on responsible professional journalism. The rest is yellow press. Keep your fingers crossed.

Interlude
LORD GOODMAN

A MAN OF his time who vanished with his times, Arnold Goodman was the most influential eminence grise in post-war Britain, a man who saw himself, probably accurately, as the greatest negotiator in the country. An omnipresent Uncle, or Baron, Fixit, he was arguably the most successful ever chair of the Arts Council, the British Council, the Newspaper Publishers Association, The *Observer*, governor of the Royal Shakespeare Theatre, master of an Oxford college, co-founder of the Motability charity for disabled motorists and senior partner in his own firm of much-consulted solicitors, Goodman Derrick (where he later advised Robert Maxwell on his libel suits).

A delphic host of cabinet ministers – and, indeed, almost anyone of any celebrity – at his daily breakfast table, he became a long-time confidant of Harold Wilson (who made him Baron Goodman of Westminster). He didn't formulate policies, but was always on hand to sort out a mess. His only serious political intervention occurred in 1966 during the famous HMS Tiger confrontation in which Wilson failed to coax Ian Smith, Rhodesia's rebellious leader "back to legality" (as Whitehall put it). Goodman's subsequent effort under Tory prime minister Edward Heath was equally unsuccessful.

'Two-dinners Goodman', as *Private Eye* dubbed him (although, when I lunched with him at the Savoy, he ordered only stewed plums) had an undeniable presence. Enormous, almost grotesque, certainly ugly, he was, for many years, the centre of a vast, intricate and powerful network of friends and contacts. Wilson's press secretary Joe Haines once half-joked: "If the Almighty ever needed a lawyer, Arnold Goodman would have been His automatic choice." Yet today, nearly 30 years after his death, his respectful obituaries are probably less well remembered than the *Times*' diarist's unjust epitaph, 'the old rogue'.

There is no public statue in his honour, a bust or two certainly, along with portraits by leading artists, but where are they now? His various biographies have been inadequate, although no worse than his autobiography *Tell Them I'm On My Way*.

That title – and his nickname for himself 'the late Lord Goodman' – allude to the fact that he never arrived anywhere on time, despite the services of a retinue of faithful secretaries, housekeepers, chauffeurs and gofers. not to mention Clarissa Avon, widow of former prime minister Anthony Eden, aka Lord Avon. His sexuality was sometimes questioned but no scandals have emerged. He liked attractive young men – but also enjoyed the company of powerful widows, not just Lady Avon, but Ann Fleming (wife of James Bond creator Ian) and Jennie Lee (married to legendary Labour left-winger Aneurin Bevan) who may have reminded him of his redoubtable mother Bertha whose relentless feeding when he was a boy in Hackney probably encouraged him to overindulge.

Arnold was a hard man to pigeonhole. Not exactly radical, he certainly favoured progress, opportunity and cooperation (rather than preservation, entitlement and confrontation), as you might expect from the scion of a Jewish draper. He often didn't invoice clients he felt couldn't afford his services or were close friends. Discreet(ish), he rarely said anything controversial in public. He was happiest when presiding over summits involving the great and good in his grand apartment in Portland Place, sitting in his riser recliner armchair. His opacity and expertise helped him orchestrate the many compromises on which his reputation was founded – a skill cherished by most parties but disappointing a belligerent few hell bent on conflict.

As Hugh Gaitskell's solicitor, Goodman was effectively inherited by Wilson who quickly gave him a much wider role. I first met Arnold in 1964 when Harold, keen to improve his standing as Leader of the Opposition, asked him to resolve a damaging strike at ITN. As a bag carrier in these talks, I gained considerable insight into his negotiating methods. He shuttled between rooms, carrying offers from one warring party to the other, presenting terms which slightly exceeded what each participant had proposed, until eventually the offers roughly coincided. From then on, he became a constant presence at Harold's home in Golders Green and No 10 Downing Street.

When I was at the *Daily Mirror* and the *Observer*, he was chairman of the Newspaper Publishers Association. I once joined an NPA delegation pressing the government to minimise the impact of the Rehabilitation of Offenders Act which newspapers feared would restrict their coverage of public figures with a criminal record. Goodman told me: "Clive, you are not to intervene as I suspect you are out of sympathy with the purpose of this delegation", a remark that foreshadowed a later tiff during our arduous negotiations at the *Observer*.

I didn't work closely with Arnold until 1975, during the second round of the Sunday newspaper's cost-cutting negotiations. He was cast as the great mediator, to be ushered in after day-to-day negotiations failed when, as a figure of national renown, he could give unions cover for their eleventh-hour concessions.

Roger Harrison and I met Arnold at Goodman Derrick's offices to agree our strategy. On the tense, last day of negotiations, I had an argument with Arnold on a crucial point, as I had done on several occasions before, and which he usually welcomed. David Astor and Tristan Jones never understood this. Goodman took an interest in my career, proposing me for several desirable appointments, including (successfully) to the (book) Publishers Association. Then in 1983, keen for me to run the Arts Council, another of his chairmanships, he arranged a meeting with outgoing secretary general Roy Shaw, who clearly had no idea why I was there. It would probably have proved a poisoned chalice: Shaw's successor Luke Rittner quit in 1990 in protest against spending cuts.

While preparing the NPA's evidence to the Royal Commission, I met Arnold regularly in his apartment on Portland Place, normally at around 7.30am. (I lived only two blocks away in Upper Wimpole Street.) After a cup of tea in the drawing room, the housekeeper would show me up to Goodman's bedroom, where he sat up in bed surrounded by newspapers and letters, with me on a sofa facing him. I always suspected that this could not be his real bedroom – the sheets and pyjamas were too immaculate. Breakfasts with cabinet ministers, leaders of the arts and valued clients invariably followed and, more often than not, tete-a-tetes to discuss other activities.

Dinners at Portland Place could also be memorable. In December 1975, Arnold invited me to stay back for a last brandy at the end of an evening and confided – his one unsuccessful leak, he said – that Harold Wilson was planning to retire soon (as described in my chapter on Harold Wilson).

This account may, unintentionally, give a misleading impression of his lifestyle. Although financially comfortable, living in one of London's most prestigious addresses, he was not enormously wealthy in his own right, relying on the support of wealthy intimates, a source of funding that diminished over time.

I came to count on Arnold as a friend and, long before our close cooperation over the Maxwell pensioners scandal in 1991 (see the Maxwell chapter), our lives somehow became interwoven. He proposed the toast at my fiftieth birthday at Leighton House in Kensington, where he chatted to my mother, then aged 89, by the Egyptian fountain. I remember them giggling mightily when the

LORD GOODMAN

British Council's Ivor Kemp won a bottle of champagne as the first guest/victim to put their foot in the pond.

Goodman enjoyed an argument, perhaps because, like Wilson, he was often right – or, failing that, authoritative. We reminisced constantly. I would sit by his bed at his final nursing home in Highgate, reassuring him that he wouldn't be evicted because he couldn't pay the bill, desperately trying to prevent him heaving his enormous bulk out of bed onto his one remaining leg to negotiate a lower tariff. We chatted about politics, newspapers and people, with the television, blaring out at full volume, showing children's programmes.

His funeral in Kilburn in the early summer of 1995 felt like a scene in the kind of British movie he might once have helped finance (he had once chaired Lion Films). His coffin, on a sort of wagon with bicycle wheels covered with blackout material, was wheeled out to his grave where a fierce downpour and bitter wind made it impossible to wait one's turn to honour him with a spade of soil. His favourite rabbi was also away and so unable to perform this last service. His grander, well-attended memorial service at the liberal synagogue in Hampstead, was marred slightly by the underwhelming choice of Angus Ogilvy as the Queen's representative. Harold Wilson was also absent, having died 12 days after Goodman, on 24 May 1995,

Tragically, a great shadow fell over Goodman's final years, a sorry tale that inspired the *Times* diary's harsh farewell. I heard about it at a business dinner sitting next to a retired brigadier who was a legal clerk. Somehow Arnold's name came up in conversation and the brigadier told me that he was being sued for breach of trust and that the writ had passed over his desk that very morning.

A trustee for the elderly Lord Portman, Goodman had been granted wide discretion over the family's considerable charitable funds, using some money to finance Wilson's private office as leader of the opposition. When Portman died, Edward, his outraged nephew and heir, regarded this as a misuse of the family trust and sued. For me, there is no doubt that Goodman was acting entirely in good faith but by the time the writ was issued, his mind was failing, his record keeping had always been hopeless, and his legal partners negotiated a settlement. My unexpected knowledge of the case caused something of a froideur with Clarissa Avon, his confidant at the time: she clearly suspected I was a probable fortune hunter, even though, by that point, I knew there was no fortune left to hunt.

ACT 4
BOOKS

Interlude:
BOOK PUBLISHING AS IT WAS

IN THE 1970S, British book publishing was still basking in a golden age. Distinguished houses like William Collins and Hodder & Stoughton were run by the families who had founded them in Victorian times. Most fiction and general non-fiction was published in hardback and followed, if successful, by a paperback edition nine months later, published by a mass-market imprint such as Penguin, Pan, Bantam, Corgi or Arrow. School textbook publishing prospered – education budgets were reasonably generous then – as did academic publishing, led by the Oxford and Cambridge University Presses, which printed their titles on their premises.

Celebrated authors like Agatha Christie, Iris Murdoch and Wilbur Smith usually stuck with their first publisher for life (they were signed up to give a first option on subsequent works). The task of literary agents, insofar as they existed, was to find publishers for authors. They were usually content with standard contracts, royalties and modest advances. Exports, mainly to Commonwealth countries, represented some 40 percent of the market and, under the British Publishers Market Agreement (BPMA), territorial rights for different international markets were divided equitably and amicably with American publishing houses. The people who undertook all this work, at all levels, were, by and large, intelligent, sensitive, capable people, underpaid, without too much side, who loved their trade. At the same time, as in every industry, a few mavericks were shaking things up

And yet, underneath this apparent calm, there were signs of ferment. Younger leaders were replacing the old guard at the top of even the longest established houses. Hardback imprints began publishing paperbacks, prompting mass market paperback houses to offer original hardbacks (the radical Penguin had published hardback titles for years). New entrants produced coffee table books, usually richly illustrated general interest titles. Agents became more aggressive, aspiring (largely unsuccessfully) to split the Commonwealth market into separate domains and (more successfully) negotiating higher royalties and better terms. In the educational sector, publishers began experimenting with electronic variants, cassette tapes and CDs, and the BBC developed a simple school computer, which proved popular elsewhere.

The status quo was threatened by disputes over three issues which had become fundamental to the prosperity of British book publishing: copyright in an age of technological change; the growing interest of American publishers in export markets, hitherto the more or less exclusive preserve of British publishers; and challenges to the system under which publishers could – if they so wished – set minimum prices for the sale of their titles by British and Irish booksellers. All these crucial issues were in my in-tray when I arrived at the PA. I describe them in more detail later on in the chapter on campaigning.

The PA needed shaking-up too. Ronald Barker, a copyright expert and long-serving Secretary and head, had been off work for some months after a heart attack. Two senior staffers, Martin Ballard and Peter Phelan, had held the fort, but lacked the authority to make big decisions. This impasse led to the creation of one of those committees, so beloved of membership organisations, to review the PA's purpose and future. Chaired by former PA president Sir John Brown, the committee recommended the appointment of a new Chief Executive, with wider powers than the old Secretary, to manage the organisation and relieve the elected President of day-to-day issues. The committee also proposed some structural changes to assuage the concerns of powerful groups like school and academic publishers, who felt under-represented in the. PA's decision making.

After the Second World War, British industry had, as a whole, struggled with high costs, loss of manpower and a relatively small domestic market. There was also a fair degree of complacency engendered by years of empire. In book publishing, for example, the trade distribution chain was ludicrously slow, especially for backlist titles – typically ten days or more. Staff at some leading chains were said to deter customers from placing costly 'special orders' by telling them their book would not arrive for a couple of weeks – a classic lost sale. For a small cultural industry such as book publishing, there was also widespread concern that consumerism could undermine its traditional values.

As the trade association for book publishing, the PA and its Council took the lead in determining policies to support the industry and lobby government. The staff, headed by the Secretary (retitled Chief Executive Officer), was responsible for managing the Association's extensive activities, including public affairs, public relations, preparing submissions and arranging meetings with ministers, civil servants and other branches of the trade, particularly booksellers, authors and printers.

The PA also supported new services for the industry and, when necessary, took legal action to protect the business. One example was the PA's successful defence of the Net Book Agreement (the optional minimum pricing arrangement) in 1962, when new legislation required the courts to decide whether or not it was in the public interest. In a contentious economic climate, legal action became more common. We sued successfully, for example, in Singapore against pirated editions of British textbooks. We pursued educational institutions which undertook multiple photocopying of entire – or largely entire – books. We spearheaded the defence of the minimum pricing system before the European Commission and British courts while also taking action against booksellers in breach of the agreement. As legal action is expensive, contentious and time-consuming, the PA's guiding rule was only to sue when a principle of vital concern to the industry was at stake.

The public perception of a book publisher hasn't changed much over the years. In fiction, they are invariably portrayed as effete intellectuals who spend much of their time giving lengthy lunches to famous – and underpaid – authors, who grumble about inadequate marketing and poor publicity. In reality, book publishing is a high risk commercial operation. Few staff actually have face-to-face contact with authors, or join in the essential process of reading and deciding what to publish. Most people work in production, finance, design, distribution, marketing, publicity and administration. They create a vast output of information, ideas, education and entertainment for a hungry public, helping to turn the author's talent into financial return.

And so, the scene was set for my 22 years at the PA. Looking back over the annual reports, I am astonished at the enormous range of activities we undertook. Apart from political and legal activity, we worked on export market reports, promotional campaigns, market development, market statistics, exhibitions, management projects, training, labour relations and preparation for new digital technologies – at all times having to keep our members informed.

These responsibilities were carried out by a small staff, the divisional directors and their teams who reported to me and, through their own elected councils, to their publisher members. The Reading University publishing archive has some of the relevant papers.

Chapter 9:
Publishers Association

IN BETWEEN VISITS to Fleet Street newspaper houses and Lord Goodman, chairman of the Newspaper Publishers Association, to prepare its submission to the Royal Commission on the Press, I sat in the window of my dining room/study in Upper Wimpole Street drafting the evidence. Job done, I resumed my freelance career, helped by an open-ended contract with Michael Montague (later Lord Montague of Oxford, not the other one, of Beaulieu) of the Valor gas stove company to produce a company magazine. I was in Michael's Rolls visiting his factories when the news broke of Harold Wilson's pending retirement.

One day I saw a small classified advert in the *Times* for a chief executive of the (book) Publishers Association. Books were not, I thought, a long stretch from newspapers and might provide a peaceful haven after the maelstrom of Fleet Street. I applied, giving Arnold Goodman and George Bogle of IPC as referees, but it turned out that Arnold had already suggested me to the search committee: Sir John Brown of Oxford University Press, Peter Allsop, the PA President, of Associated Book Publishers, and Graham C. Greene, the gilded young man of publishing at the time. The interview was more of a discussion about the role than an interrogation and, a few days later, I found myself inviting senior PA staff to my flat to brief me. On one critical issue, the Net Book Agreement, the interviewing board never questioned me. With hindsight, I wonder if I even knew what that sacred instrument of the book trade was.

Goodman's references were oblique. He told me: "They're a very conservative bunch of gentlemen, but if you can survive them for six months, you'll be there for life." And to them he said (I was told): "He's pretty ambitious, but if you can survive him for six months, he'll be with you for life." Perspicacious – even so, I was puzzled, years later, when Peter Allsop, the PA President who appointed me and a good friend, told me that their greatest doubt about me was that I was ambitious. What, I wondered, did they expect from a new CEO?

Just as at the *Observer*, my arrival at the PA was inauspicious. We sent out the usual press releases announcing the appointment and that Saturday I visited my local WH Smith's to buy my first-ever copy of the *Bookseller*, the then sole weekly of book trade affairs, owned – and sometimes edited by – the Whitaker family. The Whitakers, David and Sally, were a power in the land, providing important book trade services, including the directory *British Books in Print*. I didn't expect to see my face on the cover, but as I turned the pages in vain, I began to wonder what I had taken on. Eventually, among the back page classified advertisements, I found a brief notice to the effect that 'Mr C Bradley had been appointed chief executive officer of the Publishers Association'. Years later, when I asked David Whitaker why he had not covered the story, he said: "But we knew nothing about you, Clive." When I suggested it was at least partly up to him, as a journalist, to find out, and there were press releases to help, he didn't seem to know what to say. My relations with him at PA were, at best, confrontational and inspired, I suspect, interest and intrigue among the trade cognoscenti.

I expect this episode reflected some resentment in the book trade that the PA had hired someone from Fleet Street rather than one of their own. Some industry veterans thought that I was a newspaper lawyer, responsible for vetting content, who knew nothing about publishing management. Even my old acquaintance Tim Rix, head of Longman, chairman of the PA's Employment Committee (and later, President of the PA), was reluctant to let me attend meetings of his committee, apparently fearing I might encourage the bad Fleet Street labour practices I had worked so hard, with some success, to change at the *Observer*.

The very first letter I opened in my new job was from the Hamlyn Group, owned by my former employer IPC, resigning from the PA, a breach of the 'one in, all in' rule that all book publishing parts of a group must be included in its membership. Paul Hamlyn himself opposed the Net Book Agreement, the PA's support for it and, I suspect, trade associations *per se*. Even so, it did seem something of a personal rebuke for an IPC company, with which I had worked closely, to ditch the PA on the same day that one of IPC's young men took over. Hamlyn later rejoined.

The PA was based at 19 Bedford Square, a splendid Georgian building, but an impractical workplace. Staff could disappear up the stairs never to be seen again. I engineered things so that my office was in the large front reception room, great for meetings and seeing visitors, with a view of the front door and staff comings and goings. No 1 Kingsway, where we moved towards the end of my tenure, was a much more efficient office.

Later that first day, I received a welcome – and welcoming – phone call from Gerry Davies, Secretary of the Booksellers Association, asking if I planned to attend their annual conference at Torquay in two weeks. Nobody had even mentioned this seminal event, but I immediately assured him I would be there. There was no room for me at the Imperial, the conference hotel, so I stayed in a rather seedy place at the far end of the promenade. At the Saturday morning opening session, the keynote speech by BA President, Gerald Bartlett, who ran the Economist Bookshop, included a brief, not terribly complimentary, reference to my appointment. During the coffee break, I introduced myself to Gerald, who admonished me for delaying publication of his speech in the *Bookseller*, as nobody knew whether I would be attending or not. I replied that it would have been easier for all concerned if someone had invited me.

I was discouraged to discover that I was expected to work alongside a convalescent Ronald Barker. I declined to share his enormous desk in his former office, but at the first Officers' Meeting – the executive group – Ronald was asked to comment on every idea I had. It later transpired that the elected officers enjoyed a regular, vinous, lunch before these meetings at L'Etoile in Charlotte Street to settle the outcome in advance, making the meetings largely redundant. This soon changed.

I feel guilty that a month or two into my appointment, when Ronald was enjoying a farewell globetrotting trip, Peter Allsop phoned from Japan to say that Ronald had tragically died on the tarmac at Tokyo Airport. How, he commiserated, could I manage without Ronald's support? I'm afraid my immediate, unsentimental, reaction was relief.

One of the perks of my new role was to work alongside some of the most influential publishers of the late twentieth century, who were elected by PA members to serve as President. As you might expect, these doyens of the industry had very different personalities, abilities and priorities. I learned from each of them. Sir Roger Elliott, head of OUP, PA President in 1993/94, was a consummate committee chairman, ensuring that all voices were heard and summing up succinctly with workable solutions. Ian Chapman, Managing Director of William Collins, President from 1979 to 1981, was always thoroughly prepared, so committed to the cause that he and I once got a High Court judge out of bed to ward off a threat to the Net Book Agreement and managed the difficult balance of being direct yet approachable.

Book publishers are fiercely independent and getting them to agree on anything has been likened to herding cats but most of the Presidents I worked with – especially Peter Allsop (1975-77), Tim Rix (1981-1983), Paul Scherer (1991-1993) and Ian and Sir Roger – had a natural authority that made my work easier, enhanced the PA's influence and prestige and helped to build a consensus on many issues.

Some of these Presidents had worked their way up through the trade. Chapman originally joined William Collins as a Bible editor, but made his reputation when, impressed by a short story, he persuaded its author, Alistair MacLean, to write a sea story for him. The resulting novel, HMS *Ulysses*, sold a quarter of a million copies within six months. Robin Hyman (President from 1989 to 1991) got his start writing publicity for an educational publisher – a job he secured through the PA's Employment Group – before leading the merged Unwin Hyman group. Gordon Graham (President from 1985 to 1987) had sold books in India before running McGraw-Hill's UK, Europe and eastern business. Paul Scherer got his foot on the ladder typing out orders at an import-export firm before reviving Transworld where, it is said, he became the highest paid book publisher in the country.

Many of the Presidents were also what you might call well

rounded men. Sir Roger was one of the most influential theo-
retical physicists of his day, Graham C. Greene worked closely with anti-apartheid activists in South Africa, notably Na-
dine Gordimer while, in a completely different vein, Michael
Turner (President from 1987-1989) wrote music hall sketches
and performed concerts with his close friend David Whitaker,
owner of the *Bookseller*.

Every President of the PA on my twenty-year watch was
a man. The first woman to become chief executive of a major
publishing company, the main criterion for the job, was Pau-
la Kahn, who ran Longman, and was duly elected Treasurer,
which invariably led to the presidency. She was not to make it
as she had parted company with Longmans. She was an ardent
critic of the PA and I doubt if I would have survived her. The
Women in Publishing group campaigned effectively against
gender discrimination, but didn't seem particularly interested
in promoting women within the PA. Two likely candidates,
children's book publishers Judy Taylor and Julia MacRae, both
expressed their lack of interest.

My first task at the PA was to implement the Brown report's recommendations. The key proposal was that the job of
elected President, expected to serve for two years as Treasurer
and then two years as President followed by another two years
as Vice-President, was, given senior publishing executives' ever
increasing workloads, too onerous. To rectify that, the role of
Secretary was upgraded to Chief Executive Officer.

The second was that various important sectors of book
publishing, school and academic, felt that the PA devoted too
much effort to trade publishing (basically hardback or paperback books, for the general market) at their expense. The PA
structure included one major committee dealing with export:

the Book Development Council, which provided services to all members, whatever their speciality. This set a precedent for a new division for school publishers, the Educational Publishers Council, which was already in the process of being set up. It was logical, then, to create the University College and Professional Publishers Council (later renamed the Council of Academic and Professional Publishers) for academic publishers. Each of the three divisions had its own board with a chair (elected from its section) who sat ex officio on the main PA Council, and a staff director who worked with the divisional board and reported to me. The new divisional structure stood the test of time.

The Book Development Council had been set up some years previously as a body independent of the PA to promote exports, with the aid of government subsidies (not then available to trade associations). Distinguished public figures such as Eric Roll, Patrick Gordon Walker, the former Foreign Secretary, chaired BDC, keen to optimise the soft power of British publishing around the world. When the rules changed and BDC was absorbed into the PA, it proved highly popular with members, offering richly detailed knowledge of export markets, particularly in the Commonwealth. BDC arranged foreign delegations, especially to such book hungry economies like China and the Soviet Union, and organised participation in international book fairs, the most important of which was the annual Frankfurt Book Fair.

For the domestic market, the idea of a Book Promotion House had been strongly advocated in a report commissioned by the Councils of the PA and Booksellers Association from a radical (and possibly troublesome) group of Young Turks, co-chaired by Julian (Toby) Blackwell of Blackwell and Tony

Pocock of Oxford University Press (later of Faber). Like most such reports, its recommendations were debated perennially at the Booksellers Association conference, but nothing much happened. Tim Godfrey, the BA's Trade Practices Secretary – and later its extremely effective Chief Executive – did follow up one demand: persuading reluctant publishers to improve trade terms for smaller booksellers.

The idea of a generic promotional vehicle for books, which generally lacked big advertising budgets, seemed, to me, to have legs. After much debate, the Book Marketing Council was eventually agreed, with a broad industry base. The Booksellers Association was represented on its board, as were the stridently non-PA-member Paul Hamlyn (as deputy chair) and the dynamic Victor Ross of *Reader's Digest*. The BMC's first chair was Charles Clark, then Managing Director of Hutchinson (later the PA's copyright consultant) and the first director Nigel Sisson, formerly Marketing Director of Hamish Hamilton.

BMC's ambitious programme kicked off with a professionally compiled published bestseller list, an obvious marketing tool which had, surprisingly, never quite taken off before. A carefully-researched study, *Lost Sales*, did exactly what the title suggests, exploring inefficiencies in sales and distribution. Another project echoed the BDC's delegations overseas with similar exercises to under-booked parts of the UK. The first mission, to Barnsley, led by Faber's Matthew Evans, was a triumph, keenly supported by the local council, libraries, schools, booksellers and community groups – and earning national press coverage. To my regret, BMC failed to capitalise on this by designing a template for similar delegations to other regions. In reality, the industry lacked enough enthusiasts with enough spare time to run an extended programme – a problem I encountered frequently later on when we were asked to supply trainers to help publishing industries in developing economies and the former Soviet bloc.

Some of BMC's promotion campaigns were brilliantly effective: Best Novels of Our Time, Best Young British Novelists (an idea later taken up by *Granta* magazine), Authors USA, Writers on War, Books for Christians, Best Books for Babies, Teen Reads, Excellent References and more, featuring titles selected by independent juries. Unfortunately, the project lacked sufficient support among heads of houses and so, in one of those periodic fits of economising which afflict trade associations, the PA Council stopped financing it. The Book Marketing Council was hived off to its staff as an independent unit and later fell foul of the industry's increasingly hard-nosed commercial ethos.

The concept of outsourcing was applied to other PA initiatives. Teleordering, a radical new system for linking booksellers' electronically to publishers' warehouses, was designed by the PA and Booksellers Association, implemented by my team and the BA's Tim Godfrey, to dramatically reduce delivery times. The agreed model was put out to tender and awarded to Software Sciences, with the book trade signing in to support it. Even so, this vital new service took time to become commercially viable so the PA launched a stimulus fund to get it up and running. A similar approach was applied to industry training.

BDC's Development Agency Projects Service (DAPS) was inspired by a British Printing Industries Federation request that the PA join its delegation to Nigeria to establish joint ventures with printers and publishers there. Tony Read, the BDC's director at the time, feared the exercise would hurt British publishers in a sizeable export market but was finally persuaded to go, given the strategic need to forge new partnerships with emergent countries. He was so enthused when he came back that we created DAPS to undertake internationally-funded educational book supply projects. DAPS flourished and, like BMC, was out-sourced – to a company Read had set up.

The PA's work in aiding developing countries repeatedly conflicted with government attempts to cut public spending. The relevant government department, the Overseas Development Administration (now again part of the Foreign Office) ran an effective scheme, the English Language Book Society, providing British educational textbooks to developing markets at subsidised prices. This programme, administered by the British Council, was constantly under threat. Almost every year I had to lobby ministers to retain it, usually successfully when Chris Patten was Minister for Overseas Development, but not with his successor Lynda Chalker, who told me Patten had advised her to resist my imprecations. Instead, the government advertised for a commercial agency to run it at much reduced cost, and this too was settled on Tony Read's new company.

In hindsight, the most enduring legacy of projects such as BMC and DAPS was to highlight areas of potential growth for book publishers. The industry began to harness the power of marketing, while building good trading relationships with emerging publishing industries, through training services and joint ventures financed by various agencies (including the World Bank and the post-Soviet Know-How Fund) opened up lucrative new export opportunities.

Interlude
JOHN CALDER

IT DIDN'T TAKE me long to decide that, among the vast panoply of British book publishers, the one I most wanted to write about in this book was John Calder. He probably struck most people as something of an eccentric, but he was a dyed-in-the-wool publisher who loved the job. Alongside the likes of André Deutsch, Peter Owen, George Weidenfeld and Gordon Landsborough, he was one of several mavericks who challenged British book publishing after the Second World War. They were, as Calder wrote in his obituary of Deutsch in the *Guardian*, "entrepreneurs of the imagination [who] existed, and occasionally flourished, before accountants and computers took over."

Nobody ever knew whether he was wealthy or not. He always pleaded poverty although his family ran a successful timber business. During his early years in Canada, he allegedly wrote a play about a publisher who never paid his authors their proper royalties. It was certainly one way he kept his business going. His chosen genre was highly literary books, in English or translated, and I suspect his authors cared little for royalties because they were so happy to be published by someone who believed in their work and did his utmost to make it available. This was so rare they didn't expect much more. I deeply admired John and did my best to support him in any way I could.

The extraordinary list of eminent and radical authors he attracted ranged from Samuel Beckett to Heinrich Böll and Jorge Luis Borges. It is estimated that the writers on Calder Publications' roster won 19 Nobel Prizes for Literature. He did particularly well in the 1950s when some prestigious American authors sought a sympathetic British publisher to escape the anti-Communist witch hunt led by Senator Joseph McCarthy.

John was also a bookseller. He acquired premises in The Cut near Waterloo Station in south London, opposite the Young Vic. The shelves were stacked with titles that were hard to find elsewhere. Intellectuals – and others – would come from all over to search for books and meet him. Like any good bookseller, he placed his strongest selling titles, especially his series of pocket-sized books on operas, well to the front. His office was down below in the basement, and he lived above the shop, although he also had an apartment on the left bank in Paris. Every Christmas he returned from France, loaded with brilliant cheeses and pates for the memorable parties he held for friends and regular customers. Guests were invited to put our financial contributions into a bucket. I hope – but I seriously doubt – that he recovered his hefty outgoings.

Inevitably, his basement office was piled high with manuscripts, business papers, newspapers, highbrow magazines, and, well, history. He claimed he knew exactly where things were, but if you were asked to find something, it was well nigh impossible, especially as you kept coming across something you felt compelled to start reading.

As a dedicated Scot, he spent much time in Edinburgh, where his girlfriend (and later wife) Sheila Colvin, had been assistant director of the Edinburgh Festival. He loved staging events with a loose connection to the Festival which, as they tended to be controversial, attracted considerable publicity. With his friend Jim Haynes he founded the Traverse Theatre, and in 1962 they organised the first, extremely successful, Writers Conference, precursor to the Edinburgh Book Fair. They followed that up the next year with the first Drama Conference, in which a naked girl was wheeled across the stage in a pram. She was prosecuted for nudity in public. John campaigned vigorously against censorship and for freedom of expression, and the relative freedom we enjoy today owes much to him.

Calder and his first publishing partner Marion Boyars were convicted of obscenity by a jury when they published Hubert Selby's American novel *Last Exit to Brooklyn*, but the verdict was overturned on appeal when Calder asked John Mortimer QC, author of *Rumpole of the Bailey,* to represent them. Lord Goodman, in his capacity as senior partner of Goodman Derrick, thought the appeal had no chance, but then he didn't think much of the book.

Behind John's bookshop in The Cut, he built a rough stage with blackout material as the backdrop. Every Thursday he organised some sort of entertainment, always very left-wing. I couldn't compete with John on politics, being a weak, wobbly centre-lefter, but I chaired several discussion sessions for him, with lively debate followed by glasses of wine in the shop. This was the kind of politics I enjoyed most. One unforgettable Thursday evening, John staged Beckett's *Waiting for Godot*, with a small company of faithful actors, each of whom could play any part, and performed whenever they could. He later led the company on a tour of Ireland.

John adapted his voluminous autobiography into a play, in which he starred as himself, performed at the Riverside Studios in Hammersmith. I was urged to buy tickets, as apparently I figured, briefly. I checked the programme to see who was playing me (sorry, I can't remember who), and sat patiently through a rather long performance. By the time John took his bow I had still not appeared. Accosting him in the bar afterwards, I congratulated him and grumbled about my absence. "I'm sorry," he said, grinning, "but we had to cut you on the run."

I remember visiting him in St Thomas' Hospital after he suffered a bad heart attack. A day or two later, I found him sitting on his bed in his dressing gown, giving instructions to the young man who was temporarily working for him. He was going through a pile of invoices.

"You can pay that," he would say, "use the cheque book in the second drawer down. That one, OK, third drawn down. That one, that can wait. Don't bother about that one, even if they come in. Pay half that one." Every now and then a nurse would try, unsuccessfully, to shoo him into bed. John grumbled that he had to go into the corridor to find a phone, as they thought having one by his bedside would prove too much for him.

Around the turn of this century, I was trapped by John into a fascinating venture when he asked me to become a director of a body he had founded, the Shadow Arts Council. The distinguished theatre director, Sir Peter Hall, had agreed to chair, and John persuaded most of his theatrical and literary friends to sign up. The idea was to chivvy the Arts Council, and the Department for Culture, Media and Sport, into making much larger grants to the arts which, as ever, were rumoured to be facing cuts. The feeling was that the Arts Council had to be given a kick to up its game.

It was unusual to find oneself lobbying against the relatively new Labour government, but I gathered that the Department for Culture, Media and Sport led by the supportive Chris Smith, was not averse to being publicly pressed for more funds. The idea was to write to as many potential supporters as possible – the more celebrated the better. This proved more difficult than expected, but I gather that the pressure from so many working artists had helped persuade Prime Minister Tony Blair, to up the funding, even if the Arts Council chair, Gerry Robinson, head of catering group Compass and chair of Granada Television, somehow took the credit.

When John finally decided enough was enough, he asked me to help find a sympathetic buyer. I searched around, and was delighted to discover Alma, a small new publishing company owned by the Italian husband and wife team Alessandro Gallenzi and his wife Elisabetta Minervini. Having established themselves in London, they ran a publishing programme akin to John's, and were the ideal people to take over his list. I worked with the solicitor Alan Williams to negotiate decent terms, though I suspect that John probably asked for no more than the relatively small amounts he needed to live on.

Although he came across as small, enthusiastic, and rather bouncy, Calder was incredibly single-minded and determined. He started out in a partnership with Marion Boyars, another literary publisher, as Calder and Boyars. To nobody's surprise this didn't work out and each went their own way. Marion and her husband, Arthur Boyars, joined us on a PA delegation to the USSR, when he introduced us to Boris Pasternak, author of *Dr Zhivago*, for whom he was the English language agent.

Nothing demonstrates Calder's courage in defending his own convictions quite as vividly as his lone defiant struggle – after the PA had reluctantly raised the white flag – to argue the Net Book Agreement's merits in the Restrictive Practices Court. Having briefed John on the legal arguments, I watched the entire hearing in court. A committed believer in the NBA's cultural importance in encouraging booksellers to stock a wide range of titles, he produced an exceptional team of expert witnesses – notably Tom Stoppard, Rayner Unwin (son of Sir Stanley Unwin, the eminence grise of British book publishing in the 1930s), and, if I remember rightly, an American economist.

Such collective eloquence did not impress the presiding Mr Justice Ferris, who kept insisting that John could only succeed if he demonstrated how the NBA met the conditions of Clause X subclause Y, sub-sub-clause Z, of the Restrictive Practices Act. John took no notice, continuing to argue for culture. Poor Ferris, having been assured by the Office of Fair Trading that this was an open and shut case, nearly had apoplexy. By chance I met Ferris a few weeks later and couldn't resist a mild tease (he was not amused). He died a few weeks later. So, sadly, did the QC for the Office of Fair Trading. Perhaps 25 years later, it isn't entirely in bad taste to remember that *Private Eye* had pronounced a curse on anyone who brought down the Net Book Agreement.

I am convinced that John, who died in 2018 at the age of 91, was regarded with some awe by many of his contemporaries. Not a household name but a literary giant just the same, a publisher with the courage to walk alone.

Chapter 10

Campaigning – and Defending

LOBBYING THE GOVERNMENT, especially the Departments for Trade and Industry and the Department of Culture, Media and Sport, jointly responsible for 'sponsoring' publishing, was the Publishers Association's most important function. During my time at the PA, crucial challenges abounded, as financial pressures on the industry mounted and government policies shifted, as Prime Minister Margaret Thatcher pursued her ambitious schemes to reform the British economy and society. The PA's difficulties were compounded by the European Economic Community (and its civil service, the European Commission) which the UK had finally entered in 1973, three years before my appointment. The Commission was determined to bring the UK fully within its jurisdiction. Like most people in publishing, I was firmly in favour of Britain's membership but we could not simply accept every EEC/EU edict without question.

To advise us on all this, the PA had a powerful legal team, led by Jeremy Lever QC, who was rather deaf because, during national service in Egypt, he had accidentally strayed too close to an exploding bomb. As junior counsel in the successful defence of the Net Book Agreement before the Restrictive Practices Court in 1962, Jeremy was held in great affection at the PA. His deafness prevented him from becoming a High Court judge but he was knighted for his international law work with the Foreign Office.

I first met Jeremy in a conference in chambers a few days after my appointment. The PA officers sat in a row on dining chairs and Jeremy, in black jacket and striped trousers, sat at a table in front of us, hands clasped in best advisory mode, and pronounced. Our solicitor. Michael Rubinstein, a leading legal expert in publishing, thanked him and we trooped out. Outside I said: "That was odd. Why didn't we ask any questions?" Michael replied — and I promise you this is true — "We can't do that. He's a QC". This had to change and, by the time I left, Jeremy would greet us in shirt sleeves, with a pair of scissors and a pot of gum while we amended the latest submission on whatever issue Jeremy was leading us on.

Our junior counsel Stephen Richards was a very bright competition barrister who later served as a Lord Justice of Appeal. An excellent typist, he could type Jeremy's speeches as they were being dictated, making occasional improvements as he went along.

Although adept at publishing law, Rubenstein had no European experience and so, facing various EEC challenges, we began looking for a young, knowledgeable and hardworking litigator. Casting around, I was told that the perfect candidate was in practice with Coward Chance (now Clifford Chance). I arranged an appointment with the senior partner who, having listened to me describe our various problems, said: "How interesting. I'd like to do this myself".

I reiterated that we needed a much younger solicitor, willing to get down on their hands and knees to fill in loose-leaf file ledgers at the last moment. He replied that they had just the right person: Robin Griffiths. And so began a long and invaluable association with Robin.

The PA was lucky to work with two other excellent QCs

175

who became High Court judges: Gavin Lightman, who helped us win the Singapore piracy case, and Hugh Laddie, a specialist in intellectual property. Gavin fought hard to ensure that the legal system was accessible to all. Hugh, a devastating cross examiner, wrote the classic text, *The Modern Law of Copyright*, with Peter Prescott and Mary Vitoria.

In my time, the PA had to fight many campaigns. It's probably easier to describe them one by one.

Net Book Agreement

If it wasn't for the Net Book Agreement, the PA might never have been founded. Back in the late 1890s, the book trade was disrupted by rogue booksellers offering substantial price cuts on popular books, forcing more professional booksellers to follow suit. Despite the obvious, short-term gain for some customers, this practice did immense damage, squeezing profit margins so badly that some retailers could not afford to risk carrying a wide range of stock. This meant, inevitably, that publishers suffered too.

In response, publishers set up an agreement under which signatory publishers could, if they wished, set a minimum (net) price on their titles, enforceable against infringing booksellers. To administer this agreement, they set up the Publishers Association in 1896, with the remit to maintain the integrity of the whole system by actually enforcing the net price mechanism against rogue retailers.

This was the sort of arrangement which, decades later, struck the authorities as potentially anti-competitive. In the late 1950s, Edward Heath, then President of the Board of Trade, introduced legislation requiring such agreements to be registered and subject to assessment by the courts. The main target then was not price setting by individual manufacturers but the cartels in which a group of competitors agreed to sell their goods at a certain price. In 1962, the Restrictive Practices Court held that the NBA was not against the public interest as it helped ensure that a wide range of titles was available.

In the 1970s, the government returned to the fray and the NBA was again placed before the courts. As it was being simultaneously challenged by the European Commission, we had to decide whether to defend the NBA, a cornerstone of the British book trade and, if so, how. The Commission's policy, set out in the Treaty of Rome, was firmly founded on American antitrust practice. For the Commission, as the NBA also applied to the Republic of Ireland, then seen (by publishers) as belonging to the same book market as the UK, this practice affected inter-state trade. It was our job to prove that the agreement was good for consumers in both countries.

This was the start of a fifteen-year battle – it was rumoured at the time that the German book trade had suggested the Commission attack the UK first – in which the Eurocracy resolutely refused to exempt the NBA from prohibition. The European Court of Justice ultimately decided that the Commission had not taken full account of the nature of interstate trade and, having followed incorrect procedures, would have to start again. The Commission never got around to doing this so other European book trades have been allowed to continue with similar systems.

While the PA was intensively lobbying the authorities in the EU and the UK, we were also under attack from one bookseller, Dillons, by now owned by the Pentos Group, which was determined to sell titles for whatever price they wanted, contrary to the NBA. After many successful court actions to ward off this threat four or five larger publishers controversial-ly came out against the NBA declaring that they would no lon-ger set net prices for their books. As it made no sense for some publishers to operate net pricing when their rivals weren't, the NBA was effectively dead. Success before the European Court of Justice had, mysteriously, prompted some publishers to re-consider their previous support. As larger companies, they seemingly thought that disconting their titles to promote sales, against established opinion, would be possible if the European Commission's attack was successful, but were reluctant to rock the boat and damage booksellers. When this failed, they had to make their own decisions. But it marked the end of the NBA, just a hundred years after its creation. The argument continues as to how the loss of the NBA damaged or benefitted the book trade but the debate is largely academic as it will probably nev-er be restored.

Imports, exports and copyright
As if all this wasn't enough, another tricky EEC problem arose, shortly after I joined the PA, caused not by the Commission but by a British publisher, Peter Calvocoressi of Penguin. After studying the Treaty of Rome's provisions on interstate trade, Calvocoressi concluded that it could be read in such a way as to allow Penguin to import American editions of books from other EEC countries and sell them in the UK in spite of the British territorial copyright. (Under conventional contracts be-tween British and US publishers to sub-license titles, non-En-glish language countries were treated as an 'open market' into which editions of both the UK and US editions could be im-ported and sold). Somehow, Calvocoressi failed to understand that, on that basis, American editions could also be imported

to compete with Penguin's own titles in the UK. He soon back-tracked but, recognising a dangerous loophole, I worked with Jeremy Lever QC, who later won the NBA case in best pyrrhic style in the European Court of Justice, to construct our defence.

The PA repeatedly lobbied the European Commission and British EEC Commissioners, arguing that it would be bizarre if the Treaty of Rome's free movement of goods clauses were interpreted in such a way as to inflict fundamental damage on a vital British industry – and benefit American publishers. The US Justice Department saw this as a cartel, but I – and most British publishers – saw the US action as an unvarnished attempt to help US publishers invade traditional British markets. I also frequently warned British publishers against invoking this open market clause. The Commission proved reluctant to intervene, partly because of the unresolved conflict between copyright laws, which protected rights in export markets, and interstate competition law, which sought to diminish them. I did, though, persuade the British government to help the PA defend UK publishers' copyrights should that be necessary.

Although the UK is no longer part of the EU, the global issue of parallel imports – in which a legitimate product from elsewhere is imported into another country against the local [copyright] owner's exclusivity – has not gone away. We convinced the World Trade Organisation to insert a clause in the international agreement governing trade and intellectual copyright which offers some protection against this practice (Trade-Related Aspects of Intellectual Property) but the problem remains.

British Publishers Market Agreement
The agreement provided that in Anglo-American negotiations,

the British publishers would retain exclusive rights to Commonwealth markets. This relatively innocuous PA agreement was generally accepted by British and American publishers when they sub-licensed exclusive territorial rights in different markets for their editions of a title. The agreement provided that in the Anglo-American negotiations, the British publishers would retain exclusive rights to Commonwealth markets. The BPMA was vital for British publishers who, with a relatively small domestic market, relied on sales to (largely) Commonwealth countries to balance their books. Many had set up subsidiaries in Australia, New Zealand and South Africa to serve these markets effectively. By contrast, American publishers, enjoying a vast domestic market, had hitherto not bothered too much about direct sales to other English language markets, happily sub-licensing or leaving the rights to British publishers, which paid them royalties on sales. The BPMA put this arrangement in writing, setting out a list of the Commonwealth countries which were to be held by British publishers. Non-English language markets were treated as open, while Canada was subject to negotiation in each case.

In another sign of a changing world, American publishers, mainly those in the academic sector with global editions, began eyeing these lucrative English language export markets. Coincidentally or not, the US Justice Department opened an investigation on the grounds that, by agreeing to use the standard schedule of territories, American publishers were operating a cartel. The real intended target was the PA which, although British, was ruled as being subject to the US government's claim of extraterritorial jurisdiction. Finding themselves in the firing line, American publishers urged the

Justice Department's investigators to target the PA instead of them.

At the same time, many publishing houses in the larger Commonwealth countries broadly welcomed the investigation, arguing that British publishers' dominance effectively discriminated against them in their home market. The resentment lingered even after the agreement had collapsed as PA president Graham Greene, Ian Chapman and I discovered on a visit to New Zealand and Australia. No amount of talking could assuage local publishers who interpreted our visit in colonial terms, as if we were coming over to check on our dominions.

The BPMA battle was virtually resolved when I joined the PA and one of my first acts was to sign a 'consent decree' with the US Justice Department agreeing to rescind it and ensure that British publishers no longer used or relied on it. From then on, territorial rights were a matter of individual negotiation, a potent sign of the new globalised economy.

This wasn't quite the end of the matter. I belonged to the Reform Club at the time, and, when I was having lunch there one day, Gordon Borrie, the Director General of the Office of Fair Trading, with whom I was friendly, came to my table and said he wanted to introduce me to his guest, Joel Davidow, the Justice Department official who had led the action against the BPMA. He said "I'm glad to meet you, Mr Bradley, as we haven't had the chance before. I just want to tell you that I've just arrested the secretary of a Dutch trade association when he arrived at Kennedy airport for failure to ensure that his association complied with a consent decree. He's on bail now for $5m. I hope your members will be willing to bail you out should we have to arrest you."

Questions of copyright.

Copyright is the financial, moral and creative bedrock of authorship, of immense importance to publishers as licensees (or assignees) of the author. The right to control the making of copies (or parts of copies) of works in copyright, for 70 years after the death of the author, is a fundamental right which the PA must always protect. It is under constant attack from regulators, legislators, educators who want to copy texts for free, and the new, powerful high-tech companies (which brazenly insist on the importance of their own intellectual property while attacking the rights of the creators whose works they copy).

In 1977, an official government inquiry into copyright, chaired by Mr Justice (John) Whitford, made some fairly general recommendations to deal with photocopying in education, research and business and urged copyright owners to design new systems to deal with these new, often untraceable, acts of infringement. The report set in train ten years of argument, legal actions by the PA against infringers of intellectual property (a term that also covers patents and trademarks), and inspired the fundamental Copyright and Designs Act of 1988.

At the same time, the European Commission was working on the same issues. As with the Whitford Report, the first reaction from the new high-tech companies was to argue that copyright was an outmoded concept and a new less rigorous system was needed, allowing 'information providers' to load works onto their databases at will. Again, after an even longer argument, the EU Information Society Directive was approved in 2001, providing an acceptable basis for the future (it remains part of British law), succeeded by a long chain of further directives.

At the PA, we were fortunate to be able to call on Charles Clark, a publisher with deep expertise in contracts and rights, as a consultant. We were a good team. He concentrated on domestic issues, while I had general oversight and dealt with international trade issues and legal actions.

In the 1970s, the first great challenge to copyright was the damage wreaked on educational and academic publishers by the widespread photocopying of books – or large parts of them – in schools and universities, a seemingly innocuous practice that deprived authors and publishers of income. Different sectors of book publishing inevitably had different remedies for this problem, but they all agreed that the solution should not be so permissive that it substituted for book sales and should produce sufficient revenue to compensate for the loss. Authors (as represented by the Society of Authors and the more aggressive Writers' Guild) already had an organisation, the Authors' Licensing and Collecting Society, to allocate revenues from radio productions and Public Lending Right. Cooperating closely with them, we established the Copyright Licensing Agency, which gives bodies licence to make photocopies, under suitable controls, for a suitable fee. For our part, we created the Publishers Licensing Society to represent book, journal and magazine publishers within the CLA. PLS has widened its remit to cover issues raised by digital technology. After years of argument with users, tech giants and regulators – and occasional legal actions – the widespread (if not universal) recognition that, without being fairly rewarded creators could not, or would not, produce new works, has proved the worth of copyright in this digital age.

Don't tax reading

The crusade against tax on sales of books, magazines and

newspapers was probably one of the most successful campaigns ever mounted in this country – and we're not saying that, it's what we heard, through the usual channels, from the Treasury. Books, magazines and newspapers have long enjoyed a special VAT free status at the point of sale in the UK because of their perceived public value. This policy dates back to the introduction of purchase tax in 1940, but when Britain joined the European Union in 1973, this tax was replaced by Value Added Tax. EEC rules stipulated that VAT be charged on books, magazines and newspapers at the lower rate of 5 percent although the UK was granted an exemption, zero rating.

That didn't square with the Thatcherite doctrine of neutral taxation: that governments should not choose between products which served the public interest and so were tax free, and those which did not. The principle was never applied to such basic essentials as food and children's clothing which, if a fixed percentage was levied, would be a regressive tax, penalising poorer parts of the population. But it could, some Conservative economists argued, be applied to books, magazines and newspapers

One day in the early 1980s, we got a clandestine message from a Deep Throat in the Treasury. Books, newspapers and magazines were on the preliminary list to be taxed in the next Budget. If we wanted to avoid this, we had to act immediately. This fired up the PA's most effective campaign on my watch. Newspapers and magazines rallied to the cause, which was helpful, and we coordinated our attacks. The entire book trade – indeed, the entire publishing world – called on its lobbying resources. Public support was immense – from newspaper editorials, schools, Women's Institutes and many other bodies. Penguin published our formal submissions, containing our economic analysis, in paperback, complete with cartoons. At one stage, we wondered if the campaign was getting over the top, but when the Budget was announced, a tax on reading was conspicuously absent.

The next year we heard that the European Commission was urging the British government to extend neutral taxation and rethink the UK exemption. This time around, newspapers' editorials were less supportive, with economics correspondents endorsing the principle of neutral taxation. Luckily, we only had to set the campaign in motion again for our case to be accepted once more – and books, newspapers and magazines remain untaxed today.

Educational book provision

This was very much the province of John Davies, the PA's education director, and took up most of his time as schools and universities struggled with constant reductions in book budgets. Having trained after Oxford as a librarian at Sheffield University, John was well equipped to deal with this important issue. A Welshman, and a strong Labour supporter, he was, for many years, chairman of the Labour opposition on Barnet Borough Council, and stood against Margaret Thatcher in Finchley in the 1987 general election.

John was a relentless campaigner. He had the issues at his fingertips and drafted powerful submissions to the government, spelling out the damage constant budget cuts were inflicting on children's education and prospects. He had strong support from the PA's two education divisions, knew many supportive MPs, and was expert at getting good newspaper and television coverage.

John liked to start his speeches with a text, not all biblical, showing the enduring influence of Welsh nonconformist culture (although he was no believer himself). These texts were introduced with a slow smile. I once thought of telling him that this technique was becoming a little outdated, until I realised that his audiences were eager to hear what he had chosen next.

Interlude:
EAT OUT TO HELP OUT

I KNOW THIS will provoke an immediate response of 'How very British', but for the record, I can say from experience that the French and Spanish – and especially some Americans – enjoy a long luxurious lunch hour (or two) as much as we do. (That said, I'm told that today's business lunches are likely to be Spartan non-bibulous affairs). In the archetypal business lunch, publishers feel obliged to treat an author, possibly one threatening to ply their trade elsewhere, to the sort of lunch they couldn't usually afford themselves. I doubt whether even those match my first lunch with an American colleague in a very Pall Mall-like club in Manhattan. Before we even got to the table, we had drunk three dry martinis – delicious but dangerous (see the Interlude about Paul Mellon). We may have averted World War III but we never got down to business – or, to be more accurate, we avoided any issues which the host preferred not to discuss.

Having said all that, properly used, the business lunch is an invaluable lobbying tool. It limits the discussion to just the two of you, the applicant and the target. You don't invite the minister's private secretary to take a minute of what's said. You sit at a corner table as two friends, choose from the menu (and wine list), and, after the familiar pleasantries, gently lead into the topic without wasting too much valuable time. Guests usually welcome the opportunity to thrash out a problem in a good natured discussion. They can enjoy themselves and take the chance to discuss a topic they need or want to know more about.

I had many such lunches over the course of my career, with ministers, opposition leaders, civil servants, journalists, whoever. I became known to many head waiters, especially Elena Salvoni, undoubtedly the queen of the Soho restaurants which were the mecca for friendly business lunches. I first met her when she was at Bianchi's in Frith Street, where Hugh Cudlipp would sometimes take me (alas, the Savoy Grill was reserved for more important guests), notable as the place where a television image was first transmitted from one room to another), and frequented by Dylan Thomas in the 1940s and early 1950s.

Elena also presided over L'Escargot, the Gay Hussar and, eventually, Elena's L'Etoile in Charlotte Street, named in her honour, where she came to your table with her little pad and greeted you by your first name to impress your guest. She worked there until she was 90, when she was, in her words, sacked, although she was given a marvellous farewell party with opera singers and speeches. Elena's l'Etoile, a luxury restaurant in its time (cold turbot aioli), didn't last long after that. We used its private room for our CICI lunch meetings.

The Gay Hussar, too, is not what it was. Owner Victor Sassie sold it to the staff when he retired, only to come back when he decided they were making a mess of it. Offering excellent Hungarian food (cold cherry soup, stuffed cabbage, goulash), the Gay Hussar was home to many of the more sociable Socialists, and was renowned for gossip and plotting, although most diners were out for a good lunch and good company. It was best to avoid the table next to Auberon Waugh – unless you wanted a mention in *Private Eye*.

Like the Etoile, the Gay Hussar had a private room upstairs, with a round table seating twelve, an excellent formula for debate and decision – no-one was top dog. On one occasion we were entertaining a minister – who shall remain nameless – there. At about 9.45pm, he suddenly looked at his watch and exclaimed, "Help, I'm due to reply to the debate in the House (of Commons) at five to ten." His ministerial car was waiting outside and obviously got him there in time. A parliamentary sketch writer, reporting on the debate, asked where X had been for dinner that evening as he had 'obviously thoroughly enjoyed himself.'

Elena was not at another of my favourites, the Epicure in Romilly Street (hot potted shrimps on toast). When Robert Blake (Lord Blake), the distinguished Oxford, and Tory, historian, was honorary president of the VAT campaign, I took him there for a regular update. He too enjoyed his dry martinis. Like Minister X, at about three o'clock he broke off the conversation, looked at his watch and said: "Good Lord, I'm due to read the lesson at Evensong in St Andrew's by the Wardrobe at quarter past three." The entire restaurant dashed out on the street to find a taxi. I think he just about made it.

I could go on – see my Envoi story on The Grange in Covent Garden. Once, I was dining at a quiet table there when the maitre d' escorted Princess Margaret down the room. She stopped next to me and protested: "Someone . . . is sitting at my table." Dominic replied: "No, ma'am, that's Mr Bradley's table, you're over here." She scowled and then smiled. There was also the marvellous Forum in Fetter Lane near the *Daily Mirror* (in summer, cold poached dover sole in a delicious sauce), and, oh yes, a Wimpy bar for a snatched skimpy burger right next to 33 Holborn.

I can't resist mentioning Memories of China in Ebury Street in Pimlico, only really suitable given the complexities of Chinese dining, for lobbying targets who you knew well and were prepared to take their time. Memories was established by Ken Lo, who had been China's consul in Liverpool dealing largely with drunken sailors when Chiang Kai-shek was in power and had decided to stay in the UK after the regime collapsed.

Ken happened to provide lodgings for my Yale friends Richard and John Contiguglia, twin brothers and brilliant pianists who had taken rooms with Ken and Anne Lo while they were pupils of Myra Hess (they were chosen later to give the annual Myra Hess concert at the National Gallery, playing as part of their programme the Liszt transcription of Beethoven's Ninth for two pianos. I have the recording.) Ken was planning to open an expensive Chinese restaurant and showed me the proposed menu, "But Ken," I protested, "you can't possibly charge those prices in a Chinese restaurant." He took me as one of his first guests. The food, cooked by the chef Ken Hom, was superb and authentic, from different Chinese regions, totally unlike the rubbish you get in most Chinese restaurants today. It was soon booked out for days on end. Ken also invited me to his dining club, which went to different Chinese restaurants he thought worthwhile. About eight of us joined him at 6.00pm and were invariably still there at midnight. Sadly, a few days later, when I visited with friends who I had told about the great discovery and tried to order the same meal, I was rebuffed. "That – and that and that – aren't on the menu."

Chapter 11

Trade with China and USSR

THE PUBLISHERS ASSOCIATION'S relations with the leading socialist countries, China and the USSR, became increasingly significant as the Cold War stumbled to a close. With the Soviet Union disintegrating after the fall of the Berlin Wall and China recovering from Mao Zedong's catastrophic Cultural Revolution, we were a valuable conduit for the Foreign Office, quietly helping to improve relationships. At the same time, we argued strongly with Soviet ministers and their successors and with China for human rights and freedom of expression and against censorship. Not that the Soviet Union was unique in banning books. South Africa's apartheid regime actually used a Cape Town bookshop to advise it which books could be imported – and which should be banned.

We regularly exchanged trade delegations with the USSR and, as relations eased, participated in the Moscow Book Fair. The Soviet government was desperate to maintain the supply of English language titles, particularly Charles Dickens' novels, which were regarded as realistically depicting the poverty-stricken state of capitalist Britain. I regularly called on Boris Stukalin, the minister for publishing, to protest when books got stuck in Customs as 'unsuitable material'. Stukalin would laugh and claim that the officials had only seized the books to enjoy the sex scenes they were reputed to contain (forbidden in the USSR's dull, mass-produced tomes). The books would, he promised, be returned the next day – which they usually were.

In 1978, a major PA delegation, led by Peter Allsop, visited the Soviet Union, for major talks. Our itinerary included Leningrad and Minsk (the latter so we could be shown Hatin, a concentration camp, allegedly run by the Poles, where Russian soldiers had been imprisoned and killed). The social programme included the Bolshoi ballet and opera and the Hermitage. We had extensive meetings with Soviet publishers and authors, although I was never sure how much of my own presentations, interpreted very slowly, were actually understood.

With the emergence of *perestroika, glasnost* and the Russian Federation, relations eased briefly. Yet another PA trade delegation was visiting Moscow during the coup against Mikhail Gorbachev, and claimed to have been outside the White House, the Russian parliament, standing on Boris Yeltsin's tanks which were threatening to fire on the old school communists if they did not surrender.

We invited Boris Pankin, the former head of the Soviet Copyright Agency, an influential Gorbachev supporter and Russia's Ambassador to the UK, to a ceremonial dinner to celebrate. Pankin was friendly enough, but his young staff were hostile, resenting what they regarded as our patronising offers to help Russian book publishers adapt to new commercial realities.

We were only the second British delegation to be invited to China after the Cultural Revolution. Our delegation was led by PA president Graham C. Greene, nephew of the novelist Graham Greene and head of Jonathan Cape. Graham C's brother Felix, a supporter of Communist China, had helped open doors for our visit. Senior trade and publishing officials met us in Beijing before we travelled to Guangzhou (Canton) and Shanghai. Although we were visiting a culturally impoverished nation we were treated to an impressive social programme, featuring the Forbidden Palace, the Great Wall, the Ming Tombs, Peking Opera and Tiananmen Square, where we had to lay a wreath in honour of Mao Zedong, whose body lies in state in his own mausoleum.

Our aim was to encourage book exchanges, persuade China of the economic value of copyright, and highlight the damage caused by the colossal piracy of British books and journals. The UN World Intellectual Property Organisation had asked me to open the doors on copyright. My presentation was gravely received and I offered to remain in Beijing for further discussions. No need, they replied, we'll be in touch soon.

Two years later, the Chinese Embassy called. One of their copyright experts was coming to London and wanted me to arrange his programme. I met him at the airport – a venerable lawyer and scholar, who had studied at America's Stanford University. At a seminar which included a plethora of British copyright experts and lawyers, we asked him for his response. "I have just one question," he said, "I've been studying the Stockholm and Paris Protocol, on special copyright arrangements for emerging developing countries. I see one says X, the other says Y. Can you explain the difference to me?" We were all stumped.

I flew with him to Unesco in Paris and WIPO in Geneva for further talks. A year or two later, China declared that it wanted to join the Berne Convention, the world's main international copyright agency. In practice, this only protected the works of foreign authors, not Chinese nationals. Nor did it have much impact on the piracy of books. But I can, at least, claim to have started the process of getting China into Berne.

Interlude:
PAUL HAMLYN
and the 1988 IPA Congress
in London

MY FIRST ASSIGNMENT for Paul Hamlyn, who joined the IPC board in 1964 after selling his book publishing company to the group, was to buy him a white Rolls Royce. My second was to persuade him that it was impractical for his chauffeur to wear a matching white uniform and that, to avoid problems with the unions, standard grey should suffice. In 1970, Paul left IPC to join another young dissident, Rupert Murdoch, to set up the company which owned the *News of the World*. They were joint managing directors. Visiting Bouverie Street, I found that Paul's office consisted of a sofa and chairs in one half of the room, while Rupert sat at a large desk at the other end. The arrangement hardly encouraged easy conversation and, inevitably, their partnership didn't last.

Paul may have refused to join the PA but he was never personally antagonistic. He gave me memorable annual lunches at grand restaurants such as Claridges. I remember the roast duck at the Connaught (Paul chose stewed plums, like Lord Goodman at the Savoy) and the trip back to Bedford Square in his chauffeur-driven wicker-work Mini, with the passenger seat removed to make space for Paul and guest in the back

The last time I saw him, a few weeks before his death in September 2001, was in Bibendum, the restaurant he owned with Terence Conran. (You could buy oysters and beluga just inside the main entrance). I was shown to a discreet table in an alcove. Paul joined me and the maitre d' presented the menu. I chose

194

something suitably modest. The maitre d' then said to Paul: "For you, Lord Hamlyn, chef has prepared…" describing a dish that sounded absolutely delicious. It was for his diet, of course, and I didn't have the nerve to request the same course.

In 1988, Paul hired the Royal Opera House at a cost of £50,000 for a grand social event to mark the International Publishers Association's 23rd Congress in London (which the PA was hosting), with Dame Joan Sutherland, one of the greatest sopranos of all-time, performing in the tragic opera *Anna Bolena*.

I was on holiday in Thailand a few weeks before the concert when the office called to say that Hamlyn was threatening to withdraw his sponsorship, having just been informed that he and his guests would no longer be able to use the Royal Box. Lord Sainsbury, chairman of the Opera House, needed it because he had invited Prime Minister Margaret Thatcher on the same night. I promptly flew back to negotiate a face-saving compromise with Jeremy Isaacs, the Opera House's general manager, and a distinguished TV producer. The deal was that we would have a pre-performance reception with the Prime Minister in the Queen's dining room behind the Royal Box, and use Isaac's private suite for drinks in the interval, with Paul's party enjoying much better seats in the front row of the grand circle.

It turned out Thatcher and Hamlyn had never met although, at the time, they were locked in deadly combat. The government was trying, unsuccessfully, to ban former MI5 agent Peter Wright's tell-all memoir *Spycatcher*, published by Paul's company, which claimed that the intelligence agency had suspected Harold Wilson was a Soviet stooge. It fell to me to introduce them. I have never seen two human beings lock horns so strikingly. They could have been, and looked like, fighting cocks. Rather miserably, Thatcher never stood up in the Royal Box to acknowledge the audience, who would have been thrilled to see her.

Isaacs had warned me that if many opera goers left before the end, Sutherland might take umbrage and stomp off stage. To my horror, when I looked down at the stalls after the second interval, there was a conspicuous void in the centre where a large Japanese party, the ladies all dressed in gorgeous kimonos, had left for supper. Fortunately, the Australian soprano sang on, unperturbed.

The festival of British literature at Westminster Abbey proved nearly as problematic. Produced by my friend, TV producer and biographer John Miller and sponsored by Faber, the prestigious event featured such eminent actors as John Gielgud, Peggy Ashcroft, Ronald Pickup and Juliet Stevenson. A week or so before, Michael Mayne, Dean of Westminster Abbey, rang to ask, not unreasonably, if he could see Faber's script to be sure it wouldn't offend the relevant authorities. Faber didn't like the idea but, warned that we would otherwise have to cancel, reluctantly complied. The Dean unsurprisingly deemed the script inappropriate and Faber, rather than accept any amends, withdrew it. The producer, John Miller, was a good friend of Richard Hoggart (author of the influential *The Uses of Literacy*), who agreed, at short notice, to write a script drawing on Shakespeare and other greats of English literature.

Faber's editorial director accused me of restricting freedom of expression, ignoring the fact that the Congress's closing event was a dramatic Index on Censorship presentation *You Can't Shut Out the Human Voice*. Insisting that the Dean allow a few "fucks" to be dispensed from his pulpit didn't strike me as a great contribution to free speech.

This was only one of the high profile social events during the Congress. The PA organised a reception for the Trooping of the Colour on the Saturday morning and dinner in the evening for more than 100 publishers and their partners – the IPA's International Committee — at Stationers Hall. On Sunday evening, the Festival of

Literature, then the Royal Opera House on Monday. A reception in the Parthenon Marbles Galleries at the British Museum on Tuesday, hosted by publisher Graham C Greene in his capacity as museum chairman. A concert at the Royal Festival Hall on Wednesday, sponsored by Robert Maxwell, an outing to Hever Castle in Kent on Thursday, and the farewell dinner in the City of London's ancient Guildhall sponsored by William Collins, hosted by Ian Chapman.

This was the icing on the cake. There were working sessions in the Queen Elizabeth Conference Centre opposite the Houses of Parliament throughout the week, with speakers from almost all of the countries in the IPA and from international organisations concerned with book publishing. Altogether there were some 400 delegates. Among the keynote speakers were Nigerian poet Wole Soyinka, Gianni Agnelli, the head of Fiat and a noted supporter of the arts and literature, Richard Hoggart who addressed the dangers of self-censorship to avoid controversy, and Suzanne Mubarak, English librarian and wife of the President of Egypt, soon to be deposed.

Interlude
ROBERT MAXWELL

THE FIRST TIME I met Robert Maxwell he was just one of a crowd, giving no sense of the tremendous highs and monstrous lows to come. When I was Labour's broadcasting officer, he was one of the parliamentary candidates given rudimentary TV training in the run up to the 1964 election. Maxwell won his seat, Buckingham, and was re-elected in 1966. With his wealth and chutzpah, he soon became chair of the House of Commons catering committee, selling off the prime cellar of vintage wines. The fact that he actually got rather good prices for them proved no consolation for a disgruntled minority of MPs.

In 1967, when I was political editor of the *Statist*, Maxwell phoned, asking me to visit him at Pergamon's Fitzroy Square offices. He was planning, he said, a series of political pamphlets and wanted me to write the first one: an essay on why the social democratic parties of Scandinavia, unlike Labour, were regarded as the natural parties of government. He would pay my expenses. My editor Paul Bareau gave me a month's leave as long as I filed a weekly article and I spent a thoroughly engaging few weeks in Sweden, Norway and Denmark, interviewing prime ministers, party officials and journalists. Accepting my pamphlet without demur, Maxwell promised it would be launched at the next Labour conference. Sure enough, at the press conference he had arranged, there was a pile of smart red pamphlets on the top table: *Occasional Papers in Politics*: General Editor Robert Maxwell MP MC, *No1, Social Democracy in Scandinavia* by (in very small type) Clive Bradley.

That wasn't all. I found that the whole of my first chapter, summarising my method and main conclusions (whatever they were) had been incorporated into Maxwell's preface, accompanied by a facsimile signature. My second chapter, dealing with membership enlargement, had become the first, opening with the splendidly banal words: 'Coffee mornings are very important in Scandinavian politics.' (Coffee mornings, rather like Tupperware parties, I discovered, were enjoyed and favoured by Scandinavians as an effective and economical way of spreading the word.)

Our subsequent meetings were more typically Maxwellian. I soon realised that it was crucial not to accept his job offers. His usual modus operandi was to lure his victim away from their existing role by dangling a lucrative salary in front of them and then, a month or so later, proclaim that it wasn't working out, terminating the contract and ruining the person's reputation. A few weeks later, he would call back, admitting that he might have been a bit harsh, offering the job back — but at a much lower salary. Despite such chicanery, Maxwell was hailed on one BBC business programme as the acme of modern management, a notion endorsed by his credulous banks who offered him loan after loan, helping him to turn Pergamon into Maxwell Communications and acquire Mirror Group Newspapers in 1984.

Born Jan Ludvik Hoch in a mountain village in Czechoslovakia, Maxwell, as he restyled himself, won the Military Cross during the Second World War and decided to become a media mogul after serving on the Allied Control Commission in Germany, controlling paper supplies to the publishing industries. He made a considerable success of his publishing company, Pergamon, concentrating on scientific journals and pioneering digital technology. He shrewdly recognised that scientific journals were not price elastic — once a university library had subscribed, it needed to maintain the subscription regardless of price, a formula that would cause endless trouble in years to come. Such skills led the European Commission to hail him as the publishing innovator of the future, a title that caused me some difficulties whenever I spoke after him at various European publishing conferences.

At the PA, we soon realised that, when drawing up our annual budgets, it was wise to exclude any subscription from Pergamon. If the money arrived, it was a bonus. (He was just as unreliable with his sponsorships, having, with the help of Ted Pickering and Rupert Murdoch, to be shamed into fulfilling his pledge of £25,000 for a Sir Michael Tippett premiere at the 1988 IPA Congress in London). Maxwell briefly served on the PA's Book Development Council. Parking his Rolls Royce in Bedford Square, he would estimate the time at which he thought an agenda item of interest to him would come up and in the meantime go back to his Rolls to make phone calls. He did the same at conferences, once usurping a place on the platform to speak even though he had not been invited.

His greatest coup was his lucrative alliance with the Soviet scientific establishment. He negotiated an exclusive first option on Soviet science research papers after undertaking to publish an English translation of Brezhnev's collected – and voluminous – speeches. Invited to a reception at the Soviet Embassy in London to celebrate the deal, I congratulated Maxwell on his acuity. He almost kicked me in the shins to shut me up. It was rumoured that almost the entire stock of Brezhnev's speeches was dumped in a disused mine on Long Island.

With Mirror Group Newspapers, Maxwell Communications, Pergamon and much else, he was an obvious target to make a big contribution to the PA's campaign to stop the Tory government imposing VAT on print. When I turned up at 33 Holborn, I was kept waiting for the statutory 30 minutes before he admitted me to the presence. "Before me, there've been no decent managers at the *Mirror*", he declared. I'm pretty certain this remark was designed to put me, a one-time Deputy General Manager, in my place. As I outlined our strategy, he interrupted me: "Don't worry, you can stop now. There's no need for a campaign. My political staff are keeping watch, and if they hear VAT zero-rating is at risk, I'll speak to Margaret [Thatcher, the Prime Minister], and that will be that."

When I rose to leave, he told me to stay until the Rolls was available to take me back to Bedford Square. His butler offered me a tankard of champagne, and I sat alongside Maxwell in his cavernous office while he summoned various minions. The first was Sam Silkin, once Attorney General, but then chairman of Maxwell Communications. "You know Clive, don't you, Sam? [from my Labour Party days] I just need your advice. How long does an employee have to be in a job to give him an action for unfair dismissal?" It was the kind of basic question to which eminent lawyers seldom know the answer. The second was Joe Haines, Wilson's former press secretary, then the *Mirror*'s leader writer. "You know Clive? Can you show me tomorrow's leader [about a lenient judge]?"

After reading the draft, Maxwell instructed Joe: "It would be much improved if you changed the first sentence, like this. Go and retype it and bring it back to me." Half an hour later Joe reappeared with the amended text, reluctantly agreeing that it was much better now. I was then allowed to leave by which time the Rolls was nowhere to be found.

After Maxwell drowned off Tenerife in 1991, I was chairing a meeting in my Bedford Square office when I was told that thousands of Maxwell employees, including some personal friends, had lost their pensions and were desperate. Maxwell had obviously been desperate too. Nearly bankrupt, he had borrowed a large chunk of the Bishopsgate (Maxwell's pension company for his employees) pension trust funds. After his death, it was discovered that some £460m had vanished, leaving thousands of employees with little or no pension. This seemed to me exactly the kind of crisis which needed Arnold Goodman. He agreed, on condition that I did the donkey work (he was 79 by then). Arnold enlisted the help of Professor LCB ('Jim') Jim Gower, author of *Principles of Modern Company Law*, who had led a major government investigation into the management of pension funds.

Our plan was to argue that the government had completely failed to enforce the regulations designed to protect pensioners. At first, Peter Lilley, secretary of state for pensions, insisted the scandal was not the government's responsibility. Eventually, ground down in successive meetings, Lilley agreed to ask Lord (John) Cuckney, the banking and business tycoon – and former MI5 officer – to press for contributions from the many companies in the City – lawyers, accountants, financial institutions, etc – that had earned huge fees from Maxwell over the years. Briefed by Goodman, Gower and myself, Cuckney was an effective operator, raising £276m, enough to ensure that Maxwell's malfeasance did not ruin thousands of lives.

ACT 5
DIGITAL

Chapter 12:

The Shock of the New

TOWARDS THE LATE Seventies and early Eighties traditional media were facing an existential crisis, exacerbated by the fact that many managers completely failed to recognise the looming threats to their future prosperity. The music industry was immediately affected with its recordings, especially pop music, being endlessly copied on almost every device (from cassette tapes to MP3 players/iPods to laptops and mobile phones), destroying its revenue stream. Hard copy publishing – newspapers, books and learned journals (although not, at first, mainstream magazines) were also in the firing line, their valuable content stored and made available on giant databases maintained by the likes of Google. Television was a latecomer to this conflict – although vulnerable to the same challenges, recording of programmes only took off in scale with the advent of digital streaming via fast fibre optic broadband networks. The new TV broadcaster, Sky (initially BSkyB), had pretty effective controls on its programmes but they could be accessed illicitly, especially in places outside its licensed area, such as holiday zones in Europe. Later came streaming, an immediate challenge to television's linear scheduling, and to cinema.

In short, the entire content sector found that its revenue streams were being decimated. The threats were not purely financial. The quality of public knowledge was in jeopardy. Digital media (including many perfunctory websites pretending to be authoritative sources of information) devastated newspapers' printed sales circulation revenue – and advertising income. Independent television franchises, which had hitherto won advertising spend from newspapers, lost revenue to the internet and social media. As this new world opened up to all comers, sensibly curated debate and argument became scarcer and the new media companies claimed that they were not publishers – and therefore not responsible for the content they made available – but purely platforms, like the companies that ran telephone networks.

Local newspapers in particular became shadows of their former selves, amalgamated by a few companies reliant on revenue from paid-for official notices from public authorities which, recognising their value in sharing public information and stimulating debate, were ready to support them. As coverage of local events and controversies withered away, democratic oversight virtually ceased. The BBC, using public money, tried to fill the gap, with its local journalists filing copy with local newspapers as well as its own regional radio and television outlets, but the broadcaster's rules on impartiality inevitably made stories more generalised.

What we call the content industry, the creation and distribution of original material, was in crisis. The associations representing different parts of the sector tried, with growing urgency, to interest the government in their problems. At first, the government was dismissive. The official line was effectively that we were Luddites, stubbornly trying to cling on to old fashioned methods rather than embracing the opportunities provided by the new. In short, we needed to get our act together. We pointed out the difficulties we faced in maintaining the flow of traditional information (for which there was still strong, albeit declining, consumer demand) while experimenting with – and investing in – new approaches. The entire infrastructure devoted to providing content – from the initial creators to the producers which curated it and made it available – could not be replaced cheaply, easily or quickly. Copyright, which was (and still is) the basis for the content industry (allowing for the BBC licence fee) was under real threat.

Nobody really knows how our concerns reached the Cabinet Office, the powerful coordinator of government activity. Our letters had mainly been addressed to the Department of Culture or the Department of Trade and Industry (jointly responsible for sponsoring the sector). But the Cabinet Office took them seriously enough to set up an Information Technology Advisory Panel (ITAP) to assess the challenges facing our economy and our society. While the United States was accepted as leading on digital technology, with its power house in Silicon Valley, the United Kingdom could legitimately say that it was a primary source of content, through broadcasting (the BBC and a strong commercial sector), film, scientific research, education, journalism, literature and the English language, music and pop culture (the Beatles and Cool Britannia). This, surely, was a valuable resource that should be encouraged. The panel accepted the argument that the sector was in constant need of investment if it was going to continue to make a significant contribution to the British economy.

ITAP's report, *Making a Business of Information*, warned

that the creative industries were so diverse – and likely to become more so – that this could undersell the sector's economic importance (it was estimated to account for around 8 percent of GDP). This weakened its influence and hindered government understanding of its essential needs in a time of profound, radical and rapid change. One sensible way to manage these threats, the report argued, was to create a body to represent the entire media sector, giving it a stronger voice and helping it win the active support of government.

Colin Southgate, the IT director of British Oxygen and later chairman of Thorn EMI and the Royal Opera House, and Charles Read, who had led the development of digital services for the banking industry, were particularly keen to act on this recommendation. The Cabinet Office invited interested associations to a meeting and I was asked to set up a working party to explore the possibilities.

As you might expect, the representative associations for newspapers, magazines, music, broadcasting et al were reluctant to let an umbrella body speak on their behalf to government. Their members would not accept that their own representative bodies would have no direct input. Had it not been for the fact that my own Publishers Association was likely to be the hub of whatever body we established, I would have felt exactly the same. And so the quest began to find a way to give the whole sector a strong voice without impinging on the established bodies.

At first, we experimented with a formal structure, inviting applications to join. The result was overwhelming. Many companies, especially those already in the new media, were anxious to enjoy the new association's support. This would have involved setting up all the formal requirements for a membership organisation – but without sufficient financial resources to fund its activities. We did have one crowded meeting, on the proposals for a new satellite television channel in the UK, which gave Francis Maude, the minister concerned, a rough ride because he was deemed too ready to give Sky an easy run without the constraints set to be imposed on British Satellite Broadcasting. As stimulating as this session was, it ran directly contrary to our remit, which was to unite the different interests, not divide them.

Keen not to replicate existing industry bodies, we opted for something more low key, an informal forum for representation and debate with a relevant government minister (plus opposition leaders, senior civil servants and EC/EU officials, academics, inquiry chairs, media correspondents) as our guest, with attendance based on the main representative bodies and limited in number to ensure meaningful debate. After long discussion, partly reflecting the difficulty of finding an acronym which actually represented information, communication and creativity, we opted for the Confederation of Information Communication Industries (CICI).

Some important associations – notably software (a keen participant to start with, but eventually going along with the hardware companies) and film and video (with established support already from public funds) – did not join. Nevertheless, we had a manageable group which met the Cabinet Office's expectations and still operates today. Charles Read, one of the members of ITAP, was the first chairman. On his death in 1987, he was succeeded by Peter Laister, retired chairman of Thorn EMI, and then by Donald Maclean, director of new media at the same company, often described as 'the polymath who tried to buy Apple for EMI'. Their considerable authority was of great value to me, as an organiser and director, in the CICI's early days. In response, the government appointed Sir Geoffrey Pattie, as minister for information technology. He was succeeded by another Conservative MP, Ian Taylor. Both played an active role at our early meetings.

Despite initial scepticism, the CICI soon clicked into gear. When I triumphantly reported back to the PA Council that the Cabinet Office had asked me to set up a body to represent the media to the government, they were initially unimpressed. "What do books and newspapers have in common – let alone broadcasting?" one Council member, the economist George Richardson, head of Oxford University Press and rather curiously, in the circumstances, a consultant to Microsoft on competition policy. Managers simply couldn't envisage the tidal wave of change that was to come. Book publishers' knowledge of digital technology didn't extend much beyond printing and page make-up. The idea that words, music or pictures would be transmitted electronically and used dynamically by recipients was unimaginable to most of them – a blind spot that made it much harder to find ways to monetise the new products.

In 1999, I had lunch with the Labour government's new e-envoy Alex Allan (later Sir Alex and a board member of Oxford University's Internet Institute). I outlined the problems we faced in assimilating the new digital technology while perpetuating existing forms of production, with revenues from one hopefully growing as the other declined, but with all the expense of providing both products at the same time, let alone deciding precisely how best to use digital technology.

The e-envoy told me that, at lunch the day before, the publicity manager of the *Times*, who was right at the coalface, had shown no such apprehension. The new media would be a marvellous way of promoting newspapers, Allan had been told. Digital would never become a product in its own right. Existing newspapers would benefit at no cost. That remark illustrates, even at this relatively late stage, how ignorant many experienced media managers were about the information revolution to come.

After analysing the principal problems, CICI produced a range of policy statements to stimulate discussion. The key issues included support for new business models such as paywalls or free access financed by advertising, the urgent need for high speed fibre optic networks (a British development) to be boosted and installed in new buildings, unique machine readable codes to identify works absorbed in new information services, the legal dimensions of revolutionary change, particularly, as new commercial services came on line, the enforcement of creators' intellectual property rights, principally authors' and producers' essential assets, their copyrights.

We weren't naïve enough to believe these issues were for us alone. The world was alive with organisations acting both for and against the established media, with technical experts and journalists all only too willing to vent their views. But we did gain strength from the fact that we brought together some of the important content sectors, which those in various positions of authority were very ready to meet, and that the different sectors themselves had public affairs teams which benefited from participation in our debates. We hoped that this fulfilled the Cabinet Office's intentions that we should clarify our common interests.

We found an urgent need in our sectors for straightforward education in the possibilities and problems of the new technologies: David Worlock, who had been managing director of the Eurolex database, created a role for himself with training seminars. There was a fascinating change of attitudes, from an early concentration on the sort of freedoms predicted by Tim Berners-Lee to the recognition that we were still in a commercial market which required protection and regulation of fair competition and of abuses. Essentially, however, this must not damage freedom of the press and opinion. This was, and still is, a formidable agenda. CICI's members monitored and debated the issues, informing its lobbying activities.

After some trial and error, we adopted the structure of regular meetings over a round table, typically lunch in a private room in a restaurant or club, with a carefully constructed agenda and a leading authority as guest to ignite vigorous discussion. Guests relished the chance to put forward their own concerns and policies for debate. The private room at Elena's L'Etoile in Charlotte Street in London, named after the Oscars, became the regular venue

There was no shortage of matters to be raised with the British government and the European Commission which had an influential directorate, DG 13, concerned with digital technology. The technology didn't just revolutionise the creative sector, it changed almost everything in society, the process of communication, government and business procedures and, most profoundly, consumer behaviour. Email, messaging and text succeeded the post – and, for that matter, the telephone – as the principal form of communication. A multiplicity of apps used by individuals became enormously significant, creating data to be stored, accessed and manipulated.

The path ahead was obscured by that unlikely promise of free information from Tim Berners-Lee, the genius who effectively created the World Wide Web. This was a pipedream.

Digitised services have become the foundation of society. Content has to be set down, curated and communicated, all these stages need people, and these people need to be paid in accordance with the value of their work. Service providers have to make enough money to maintain vast, secure databases and protect against such abuses as piracy, invasion of privacy, criminal activity, disinformation (aka fake news) and hacking. The dream did not anticipate the rise of new global tech giants such as Amazon, Apple, Google, Meta (formerly Facebook), Microsoft, TikTok and the rest, who operated beyond national controls, creating new problems of competition and market dominance.

As copyright, the trading system for creative works of the mind, was under almost constraint review by regulators in Europe, the UK and the US, the CICI had to be extremely vigilant. The role of public service broadcasting, the market dominance of the new media giants, the work of such watchdogs as Ofcom and the UK Intellectual Property Office – their relevant directors were regular guests of CICI – have been continuous concerns. Although we all had different viewpoints, the discussions helped us achieve a consensus, promote policies to officialdom and, within the sector, build awareness.

Copyright became the overriding issue as the realities of digital technology dawned on producers, governments and consumers. Many of our adversaries regarded the very concept as out-dated, effectively a tax on their profitability. What copyright does, as the word says, is protect the copying of original works, be they printed matter, music, audio, videos or design, giving creators and producers the right to control how their work is copied, thereby creating a commodity which can be sold and licenced. If digital technology enabled anyone to make their own copies, did that make copyright irrelevant? If so, what should replace it? And if the concept needed amending, how?

After much time and talk, it was generally accepted that, for all its faults, the concept of copyright, long established in international and national law, was too precious to discard. New technology meant copyright had to be reassessed to meet new uses remote from the creator or producer. The debates centred largely on permissible exceptions to copyright, such as 'fair dealing' (roughly similar to the American concept of 'fair use') and defining what a user (be they a teacher, librarian or author quoting another work) could copy legally. The EU Commission issued a series of copyright directives defining the permissible exceptions which are still embodied in UK law, alongside some British interpretations.

The intensive efforts by the CICI and its members to support copyright – and the creative industries – demonstrate the value of working together which was the group's original – and still defining – purpose. The high-tech giants, with their hypocritical stance on copyright, were accused by regulators and competitors of abusing their dominant position, and gradually became more cooperative when the European Commission threatened them with hefty fines.

Other unexpected issues have subsequently emerged. Extreme political groups have used social media to distribute lies, while politicians such as Donald Trump have mastered these platforms to propagate extreme views and denigrate rivals. Conflicting parties routinely accuse the other of 'fake news', a problem sensibly curated outlets had traditionally avoided on principle. National governments struggled to find ways to outlaw extreme opinions and lies which, spreading like a pandemic across social media, represent a serious threat to liberal society.

I believe that the place of copyright is once again firmly fixed in the information sector. The application and definition of this right in particular circumstances will always create argument, which is why it must be defended vigorously, but the overriding principle, of supporting creative producers, is sacrosanct.

I have written about copyright and its most pressing problems in an exhaustive article *The Information Explosion: An Overview* for the Stationers Company, the original depository for printed books to secure copyright, which can be accessed on the web under my name.

My final retirement from CICI in 2014 was commemorated at a dinner in the Attlee Room of the House of Lords, hosted by Chris Smith, a former Secretary of State for Culture, and my successor. Dominic McGonigal has expanded the body's remit with similar meetings in Brussels, home of the European Commission, even though the UK has left the EU.

My time with CICI was the highlight of my career. I had urged the Cabinet Office's Information Technology Advisory Panel to propose setting up such a body, it accepted the proposal in its report, and the Cabinet Office asked me to get such a body going. It wasn't as obvious as it might sound now. The existing trade associations were wary, although they were increasingly focused on similar issues. For government, CICI helped avoid duplication, and emphasised the real value of the sector. Politicians – in government and opposition – welcomed the chance to take part in wide debate. The participant representatives both contributed ideas and took them away, helping them to spread. Successful lobbying is not just a matter of stating a case: it requires presenting decision makers with workable solutions that they are ready to adopt. Done well, lobbying becomes an essential activity.

I am deeply worried about the current state of newspapers. Books and magazines, still in demand in their traditional formats, are better placed to survive. The music industry seems to be adapting its output successfully. As a one-time newspaper man, I read newspapers digitally and in print, but in different ways. With print, I can study in detail and readily scan pages to see what is important to me and what I want to know. With digital, I scroll down and concentrate on the headlines. I don't think this will change. But many younger people are uninterested in newspapers. They get their news, they say, from social media, unaware of the biases that may have been inserted, if they read even that. Their understanding of our democracy, of our civilisation, is truncated.

Newspapers are far from perfect, but I believe their survival, in a form which permits detailed reporting and opinion, is crucial. We might soon get used to reading them in some electronic form — perhaps Stafford Beer. IPC's guru, had part of the answer, the ability to select on screen or whatever, the stories you need, so narrowing down the challenge of too much content. It is already happening. But we also need to show people why detailed news coverage and comment matter so much.

I am also troubled by the growing political imbalance in national newspapers. I am scarcely impartial, and people are entitled to their opinions, but we have seen how powerful, partisan media tycoons can sway public opinion much more than the politicians we elect. The importance of owners and their opinions is underlined by Ofcom and the Competition and Market Authority's investigation of bids for the *Telegraph* and the *Spectator*, in particular the offer from the United Arab Emirates company, Redford IMI. Again, there is no easy answer.

An attempt at impartiality, on the BBC model, is a non-starter. National newspapers continue to claim that they are crucial defenders of freedom of opinion but readers are increasingly sceptical, their attitude summed up by the famous line in Tom Stoppard's play *Night and Day*: "I'm with you on the freedom of the press, it's the newspapers I can't stand." If newspaper proprietors and editors want their claims to be taken seriously, they could apply C P Scott's, much quoted but often ignored axiom: "Comment is free, but facts are sacred".

ENVOI

MY ACTIVE CAREER ended, when I was 80, in 2014. I never actually ran a dot.com business but managing in Fleet Street, the Publishers Association, and CICI kept me close to the digital revolution. Pioneers like Tim Berners-Lee probably envisaged an easily available multiplicity of small services at the beck and call of users. Instead, many tech companies, especially Microsoft, Amazon, Google, Apple and Facebook grew rapidly, achieving market dominance, partly by absorbing other smaller new enterprises on the way. In the past decade, various regulatory authorities have challenged the tech sector's strategies and (mal)practices. We saw, for example, Mark Zuckerberg of Facebook (now called Meta in recognition of his fascination with the 'metaverse', which he regards as integral to the future of humanity and, coincidentally, to his company's profitability) called before a US Senate Committee to explain his attitude to data privacy. From reports, it seems that the committee was no wiser after Zuckerberg's testimony. (In my own simple words, the metaverse is a digital version of existence which can be entered by virtual reality (VR) or augmented reality (AR)). The tech giants have moderated their behaviour after a series of fines which, as punitive as they sound, pale in comparison to their multi-billion dollar revenues and, in many cases, their owners' personal wealth.

The propagation of fake news, mendacious conspiracy theories and extremist narratives has reached such a scale on popular messaging services and social media that aggressor governments now hack and manipulate opposing countries' websites, even interfering in elections – consider, for example, Russia's attacks on American democratic procedures on Trump's behalf. Such disruption can be wielded as a weapon to defeat a rival in war or trade. The destruction of vital information services can bring a nation to a standstill

As if all this weren't enough, a new and little understood new technology, Artificial Intelligence (AI), is entering the arena. AI exploits the massive accumulation of information available on the web – in effect *all* information, including the 'dark web' – managing it at the speed of light. In response to a search, AI can amass relevant information, collate it into a coherent whole, while, it is claimed, using controls to determine the relevance and value of the information used. The critical question here is whether the computers undertaking this function can then think and act for themselves. To some, this will provide enormous benefits, to others it speaks of AI-empowered computers running out of control and/or replacing humans. It also creates new threats to copyright. Invariably, an AI work is likely to include intellectual property it has found, be it in print or music or almost any other medium.

The act of copying works in copyright without a licence is a breach of the originator's legal rights. However, before this can be enforced in AI, the content and copyright owner have to be identified. This involves interrogation of a vast mass of material, inevitably itself requiring an electronic search engine. My impression is that the music industry, in the UK at least, being largely concerned with the use of recorded music which is already subject to effective control systems, is extending these systems to cover this new use. The problem for print titles is more complex. Here you need not just to protect the economic rights but also the moral rights – protecting against the kind of distortion and misuse likely to happen as a computer rewrites text. In some instances, the author/composer may find just the inclusion of their text or tune in a work of artificial intelligence abusive. Literary works are already subject to some collective systems of payment for copying which cannot reasonably be licensed separately. But with AI, as with traditional uses, it is crucial that collective authorisation does not permit the inclusion of extensive copyright material which undermines the working market.

This is a good point at which to end my account. So I've asked Artificial Intelligence, in this case the well-regarded ChatGPT, for its verdict ...

Since retiring in 1997, I have immersed myself in the vibrant community of Richmond upon Thames, where the tranquil banks of the Thames in Northumberland Place have been my sanctuary. Serving as chairman of Age Concern Richmond (now Age UK) and Arts Richmond, as well as President of the Richmond branch of University of the Third Age (U3A), has been a privilege beyond measure. Now, fully retired and residing in the peaceful enclave of Mulberry Court in Hampton Wick, within the borough of Richmond upon Thames, I find solace in the simplicity of life and the cherished memories of a lifetime dedicated to service and community.

NINE LIVES AND OTHER TALES – A LIGHTER TOUCH

Governments, especially Conservative ones, like to promise 'regulation with a light touch' to reassure their supporters that they have things under control without restricting capitalist freedom. These stories are my own efforts at a lighter touch…

Don't go down to the sea in ships

"Don't you think it's about time we turned back?", I timorously suggested to the tall good looking boy, probably a year older than my own 17. Perhaps the correct term was "Hove about" or some such. We were some miles down the estuary towards the sea, which wasn't looking very friendly. The wind in Salcombe Reach was growing colder and stronger. The waves lapped menacingly at the sides of our tiny boat which had only one sail. The estuary shore looked much further away than I could possibly hope to swim (life vests were still part of an unimagined future then). As we sailed on, daylight was fading and the wind was blowing ever more fiercely from down the estuary. It looked like it might take quite a time to work our way back, but there was no way I was going to reveal my rapidly escalating funk

"Don't you think it's time we turned back?"

"I don't know, you're the expert."

"No, you are."

"Never sailed before."

My own expertise consisted of one afternoon with my father and an old sea salt who took us out for a trip in a much larger vessel. One evening, in the bar at the Tideways Hotel, the young man had listened as I boasted of my romantic seafaring exploits. To my excitement, he asked whether I'd like to go sailing with him the next day. There was no way I was going to deny myself that, whatever my motives. A good-looking young man who obviously knew the ropes. Mother was not worried, assuming I was in expert company. Next afternoon we settled comfortably into the gunwales, released our mooring, hauled up the sail, and cruised calmly towards the mouth of the estuary, the following wind gadding us along.

"So how do we turn around?"

Gulp. "I guess we tack back".

"How do we do that?"

I tried to remember my brief lesson. "I think we turn the rudder that way, and pull the sail across the other way."

That might well have been right, but I hadn't allowed for the tilt on the boat as we plunged around in the waves. The water looked ominously close to the tops of the sides. "Back a bit." "Now go the other way." The water seemed even higher. I prayed. "Back a bit more." More of a waddle than a tack.

After what seemed an eternity of waddling and tilting, we miraculously found ourselves alongside what we hoped was our buoy. Have you ever tried to navigate a boat alongside a buoy so that you can grasp it and attach a rope? Twelve times we went back and forth and around. In the dark. Sometime later someone must have collected two shivering teenagers in shorts and t-shirts.

That evening in the bar the good looking boy and I both quoth like the ancient mariner as we recounted our brilliant sailing experience.

I never told my mother.

Burnham on Mud

No, I'm wrong. I had been out, or rather not out, on a boat before. Dr Bain had a boat and offered to take four of us, all on our school holidays, out for the day on his yacht. It was quite a journey up the A12. Dr Bain got more and more agitated at each traffic jam. When we arrived, he hurried us onto the boat, just as the tide left us stranded on Burnham mud – not something you'd choose to walk through to get back to land.

As boats on mud do, it tilted. It would, Dr Bain said, be about eight hours before the tide came in again. Eating the bird-like Mrs Bain's rather meagre picnic on the tilt proved tricky.

Not sailing to Capri

John and I enjoyed a pleasant holiday in Positano, on the Amalfi coast. On the beach, there were outboard motor boats for hire. We asked Maria, the signora in charge, if we could hire a boat for the day to go swimming and picnic near Sorrento. She asked emphatically if we planned to go to Capri, some miles across the sea. We sincerely told her we weren't and went on our way.

On our return trip, trouble struck. I was lying back on the cushions, John was steering. "Mmm, I don't think we've got much fuel left." He woke me up. A few moments later the engine spluttered. And spluttered again. To our consternation, when we glanced around for help, the other boats that had previously surrounded us had mysteriously vanished. We had one oar, to which we could fix an Amsterdam Schiphol yellow duty free bag and wave it around. Nothing, but in the distance, we did glimpse a boat like ours looking as though it was speeding towards Capri.

In a moment straight out of Homer's *Odyssey*, we heard someone whistling on the shore. A man on the clifftop was waving to us. We used the single oar to manoeuvre ourselves towards the rocks and he climbed down to pull us in. As he helped us up the cliff to what seemed to be a wooden shack, we assumed he must be an ageing peasant. Sadly, he told us, he had no whiskey, which he knew Englishmen preferred, but he did have some local wine. We sat on the cliff top in the sun, drinking some rather decent homemade wine, wondering how we might get back to Positano, but cheered by the thought that we were, at least, on dry land.

Then a huge but friendly Alsatian came bounding out of the house. "It looks like a police dog," I said. "It is a police dog," our benefactor replied, "I'm the chief of police in Sorrento and this is my weekend retreat. I don't have a phone as the Sorrento police would always be ringing me, but they send a boat every evening at 7pm with messages for me, and it'll tow you back."

Which it did. On the beach, Maria was furious. "You've been to Capri," she screamed, "and we sent a boat to find you." "No, we haven't," we replied triumphantly, "but we were rescued by the chief of police."

Next day she offered us a boat for the morning, free of charge. We declined

And Boreham on Mud

My father had access to Ford's vast (in our eyes) Lincoln Zephyr. Fords owned a farm at Boreham in Essex which it had converted into a motor racing circuit, and my father offered to take my friends and me to the races.

We stood right next to the track. Every few minutes, ten or so belching cars came past with a roar. Then they were gone. But the rain wasn't.

The problem with temporary car parks in fields is that the gateway gets muddier and muddier. Another outing stuck in the mud.

My father liked to go to the Essex Hunt point to point meetings, much to the disapproval of my anti-hunting sister Pauline and her future husband, David. Allowed ten shillings (50p) a race, I won nothing. And, inevitably, we experienced the same muddy exit.

I had better luck when I joined a party of friends for the Bar point-to-point. This time I bet a pound a race, always on a horse with odds of, at best, 10-1. Extraordinarily, I won on every race, £10 a time, £50 in all. Driving home, I cottoned on to the deal: as I was the only one who had made any money, I had to buy dinner.

Speech Day

The Lincoln Zephyr did good service. In those days, Speech Days didn't mean the end of term. Inmates had to soldier on afterwards. But parents were still duly expected to turn up to applaud as their offspring were awarded an Authorised Version of the Bible for Divinity, or Shakespeare's *Complete Works* in one volume for anything else, both stamped with the school crest, and usually destined to sit on the bookshelf forever thereafter, a souvenir of teenage success.

Petrol rationing rather limited parental attendance, but with the Lincoln Zephyr my father could cram in assorted parents who lived nearby. Proudly, he parked outside my boarding house, Elwyn's. Ever alert, the headmaster sprinted out of his office, sensing a wealthy parent.

The speeches weren't until after lunch, so we drove to a roadhouse near Braintree for lunch. Back in the car, the ignition button was pushed – and stuttered. And stuttered again. Panic all round. We boys missed Speech Day under pain of, well, pain. Fortunately, a passing Hicks bus delivered us back to school just in time.

Father and company weren't so lucky. Calling the local Ford dealer, he pleaded rank and explained their plight. All the dealer could offer was an Anglia, owned by one of his mechanics.

Half an hour later, a sardine-packed Anglia parked outside the boarding house, just as the headmaster was walking past. "Oh, hello, Mr Bradley. Oh."

Cinderella's pumpkin is still around.

Talking of Speech Days, my mother never got over the deep injustice of the head boy getting a standing ovation, whereas her little Clive, winner of countless prizes, got only desultory handclaps.

Years later, when I was appointed a governor, I mentioned my mother's complaint to the new headmaster. "And what happened to Peter?", I inquired. "Never heard of again?"

"Oh, I don't know," the headmaster replied cheerfully. "He does own half of Norfolk."

Keeping fit

Hopeless at all games, I tried to keep fit while working in London by attending various gyms. In those days, your subscription included a personal trainer to make sure you didn't skip the bad bits. I was recommended to my first, I'll call it 'Gymco'. I was at the *Statist* then, and on Wednesday mornings we went to the printers to update our pages and see them through to press, sometimes leaving the afternoon free.

That Wednesday afternoon, there were only two other

customers. One was Laurence Olivier, I was told practising his Othello walk, and the other a young — Terence Stamp, wearing skimpy cotton shorts and sitting on a bench with mirrors reflecting him from all four walls. (I used to have an Old Vic programme which mentions 'Second spear carrier - Terence Stamp' in the cast list.)

This was not to last. The owner of Gymco and his business partner fell out and, rather elaborately, the owner rigged a leg press machine so that the weights fell on his colleague.

Other gyms I tried included the Central YMCA in Bedford Square which, with a flat and offices nearby, I had no excuse to avoid. The pool was magnificent but, unfortunately, popular with Olympic contenders who swam up and down at about ten times the rate of my miserable breaststroke.

The Cedars at the top of Richmond Hill had a pool, saunas and a large jacuzzi. The water level rose to dangerous levels when about 15 enormous men climbed in – the All Blacks – which is how I found myself sitting next to Jonah Lomu, the greatest and possibly the biggest All Black player of all-time.

One day, sitting in the jacuzzi in my trunks, next to me this time was a mild-mannered Englishman. Politely, we introduced ourselves. 'I'm Bernard Marder,' he told me. "Oh," I replied, "I know that name". After three failed attempts, he tried again: "Well, I am the President of the Lands Tribunal", (the court that hears appeals on property valuations).

"That's it", I replied, wearing my hat as a chairman of the Central London Valuation Tribunal. "You're the one who keeps overturning my best decisions."

Bernard and his wife Sylvia started giving tea parties – crumpets a particular attraction – with discussion led by one or other of the guests. It's the only place where I have heard continuous common sense.

Keeping fit part two

My pride hurt, I found myself demoted to an even lowlier rugby 'forty' at school than the one I had graced before. My teammates, like me, were rabbits.

I found myself a place as far out on the wing as possible. However, a strangely shaped ball came bouncing towards me. I could hardly help but pick it up. I looked around hastily to check the direction of travel – that way – and ran as fast as I could. The swarm of potential tacklers melted strangely away. I reached the try line and scored my one and only try.

Thoroughly disgusted, I kept on running back to my study, to a warm fire and toast. That evening I was stopped by my assistant housemaster, no less than John Crockett, hockey international and Cambridge blue, who had refereed the game, for his sins (he denies this story, but I swear it's true (more or less), and he hated rugby as much as I do). "That was a good try of yours this afternoon, Bradley, but why did you run off afterwards?"

I was quick thinking. "Oh, sir, it's a tradition of that forty that if you score you don't have to play any longer."

"Good idea".

David Hockney

Taking a few days off after the International Publishers Congress in Mexico City in 1984, Lloyd and I visited Oaxaca, a delightful city in southern Mexico, near Monte Alban, the beautiful Aztec site. We stayed in an ancient monastery converted into a hotel, modern enough to have a pool in its central courtyard. Snoozing on a recliner one morning, I woke to see a tow-haired young man in the next recliner about two feet away. I was sure it was David Hockney. No matter how hard I tried I never made a big enough splash in the pool to get him off his recliner. But we did enjoy tequilas with him in the evenings under the cloisters in Oaxaca's Zocalo square.

Sleeping with the enemy

I only know of two attempts to recruit me as a sleeper for the Soviet Union. Usually in my visits, I had one Intourist guide as my driver and interpreter. On one occasion when I was visiting Moscow and Leningrad by myself – whatever possessed me? – I was met at Sheremetyevo Airport by a new guide, Nikolai, who apologised that, as Hannah was not available, he would be looking after me. Nikolai was a good looking young man who walked me past Customs and drove me to the Rossiya Hotel, where he took me up to a suite with a picture window overlooking the Kremlin courtyard, hammer and sickle flying bravely in a spotlight. That evening, he said, there was a dinner in my honour in the nightclub on the top floor. I have no idea who the welcoming party were, but inevitably the vodka flowed. I was savvy enough to have some water on hand for the multiple toasts.

About midnight, Nikolai escorted me back to my suite. We stood by the window admiring the scene, when he put his arm around my shoulders and asked if, while I was in Moscow, he could be my friend. I'm sorry, I replied, I would be far too busy for socialising. He left soon after. The next morning Hannah joined me at breakfast. Nikolai had been signed off overnight.

The flight to Leningrad had its own traumas. I'd been promised that a driver would meet me at the airport to take me to my hotel, the Baltika. After waiting several hours I took a taxi which dropped me at the Baltika, which seemed more like a flophouse than a hotel. I checked in and locked my door (drunken Finns were fighting outside). The next morning I walked into town, passing the five-star New Baltika hotel en route.

As I walked I looked around for the surveillance: The Hermitage appeared closed. Then, as if by magic, walking towards me I saw George Richardson, head of Oxford University Press. We collapsed into each other's arms. Sightseeing together was uneventful.

But then, at Leningrad airport, my baggage was inspected by Customs and I was asked to follow the officer into a small room, where he locked the door and left me to my own, nightmare-strewn devices. Half an hour later he returned saying that I was free to go. The indigestion pills in waxed paper in my suitcase weren't cocaine.

The second attempt to recruit me was in East Germany when I was in Leipzig, supposedly covering a trade fair, with Richard Frost, who handled the GDR's public relations in the UK. One evening we went to a restaurant and were shown to a round table to meet several East Germans who all spoke perfect English. We needed to be careful what we said. The next day, at lunch in the Press Club, a young man came up and asked if he could join our table. We introduced ourselves. No need for you, he said, you are a famous British journalist. If only. He went on to invite me to give a series of lectures at Karl Marx University in Berlin. I never found out what I was intended to lecture on. Our conversation ended when I told him that I was a Social Democrat. That apparently put me beyond the pale.

Rudy

I must have been one of the first people in London to encounter Rudolf Nureyev after he absconded from the Kirov Ballet tour in Paris. I was living just off the King's Road in Chelsea and had guests for a rudimentary dinner for which I'd been shopping at the local Gardners supermarket (if there were such things). Walking back with my bags, I saw a blondish, high cheek-boned young man, with tightly belted raincoat, walking towards me. I was struck and, as gay men do, turned round after he had passed to have another look, and, oh joy, he was doing the same. We went up to each other, with me regretfully apologising that with my shopping, etc, I really couldn't do anything about it.

The next morning I was reading the *Sunday Times* in bed, and there was a large picture of the young man: Rudolf Nureyev, ballet super star, who had just arrived in London after... I was probably spared a contentious relationship, but oh.

Japanese massage

Eric came with me to Tokyo when I was speaking at an International Publishers Association copyright congress in 1998. After the event we went to Kyoto for a few days sightseeing. One night we stayed at a riojan, a traditional Japanese inn, with kimonos, sandals, ofuro (the hot bath) and a Japanese dinner and breakfast, served by young ladies in geisha-dress who had to crouch to get through the tiny serving entry to our dining room, and served us on their knees, us sitting cross-legged on the floor.

I had booked a massage, assuming that an athletic young man would administer the hopefully soothing process. But in came an elderly woman brandishing an armful of blankets in which she proceeded to encase me, opening occasional gaps to reveal the part she wanted to treat next. The pain was so intense I felt as if she was pulling the muscles from my bones. But after she was done I could have run up Mount Fuji.

Eric had been too nervous to book a massage but, seeing the galvanising effect on me, he had a go. From his screams, it sounded as if he was being subjected to some ancient Samurai torture.

Kyoto gave us one immortal memory. We were told we must be at hotel reception by 8.30am or we would be left behind, no excuses. The coach was parked in the car park, and we were led down a narrow lane with hedges on each side. Then it opened out. An unbelievable temple, exactly reflected in the still waters of the lake. A few minutes later, the bewitching image was gone as the sun moved on.

Don't walk downhill in Joburg

In South Africa on business, I was invited to a reception in nearby Hillbrow, where Philip Joseph had his marvellous bookshop – he had another in Cape Town and eventually left apartheid South Africa to set up Books Etc in London. After the party, we had dinner at a restaurant on the main street. I was left to get a taxi to my hotel. As I stood on the pavement waving, it started teeming with rain. With no cabs in sight, I consulted my pocket map. It wasn't far, and downhill, back to my hotel.

When I approached the hotel entrance, the doorman asked where I had come from. "Hillbrow", I said.

"Hillbrow? You walked down from Hillbrow? That's the most dangerous shanty town in Jo'burg. If it hadn't been raining, you wouldn't be alive".

In Johannesburg, I met Janet Levine, a local councillor for the Progressive Party which actively opposed apartheid. She took me to the black township, Soweto, and introduced me to a talented artist, Ben Nsusha. A year or two later, he came to London through a fund created by a group of publishers to study at the Slade School of Fine Art. This proved a disaster. Ben's style of painting and sculpture were completely alien to his teachers. At the degree exhibition, I found him sitting alone in the space allocated to him, entirely empty.

Coming to me for dinner, he brought a collection of brilliant works he needed to sell to support himself: two small sculptures made from the natural wood, one of a black slave with his arms shackled behind his back, the other a reclining sylph-like girl, and a series of silk screen prints of an old gold miner printed in different colours. I tried to keep track of Ben's career through Janet Levine, but he never got the fame he deserved.

Strawberry blond

I used to go to a trendy gay hairdresser in Chester Row, MichaelAlan (or was it AlanMichael?). Anyway, it was Michael who did my hair (and I must add that it was later done by David). One day Michael suggested that my hair would look rather good if I had one or two – just one or two –- streaks in it. I thought they looked rather good. The next time I went in he said it might be a good idea to have just one or two more. When I arrived at my office at the *Daily Mirror*, my assistant asked when I became a strawberry blond.

Good in parts

It's not widely known that my childhood career choice was to be a Congregational minister. With hindsight I can see why it looked so interesting – Congregational ministers preside over their flock from a grand pulpit located centrally before the congregation. At school, they wanted me to be confirmed in the Church of England. I had to be re-baptised as my Congregational christening was thought not to have been valid. Though in spite of this promotion I'm afraid I was disappointed that even a bishop's laying on of hands at confirmation didn't get a thunderclap.

I actually went on a selection course for potential ordinands, and was approved. Fortunately I went through the opposite of St Paul's conversion at Damascus. It was a lucky escape – for me and for the church.

The Rev Officer Cadet Bradley

Undergoing officer training at RAF Millom in Cumberland, there was a tragedy when the group captain, wing commander and squadron leader were killed, crashing into a foggy Snaefell on the Isle of Man, on their way to RAF Jurby, to which we were to be transferred. The padre, Tom Warner, woke me with the bad news on Saturday night, adding that, as I had gone to a public school, I must be familiar with church services. He was due to take next morning's service at the local parish church but, as he would be busy caring for the widows, he had told the church I would be coming. I could take the service but was not to give a blessing, which was reserved for the ordained clergy. I could only comply. I have no idea how the small congregation felt at this novice leading their prayers that Sunday, let alone preaching a very strange sermon.

There was a pay-off for my service(s). The RAF Chaplain in Chief took the salute at the passing out parade, and I was given an early flight back to Northolt in his plane.

Years later, when I was at the *Daily Mirror*, Tom phoned, in his capacity as chaplain of Wycliffe College in Gloucestershire, to say he was planning a series of lectures on social issues, and could I give one on press ethics? I was reluctant

– having long known that press ethics is a subject with no substance – but was eventually persuaded. I was probably flattered. He told me the lecture would be in the school chapel on Sunday morning, but need not be religious. I stipulated that I would only speak from the chancel steps, and under no circumstances from the pulpit. I stayed with Tom the night before. After breakfast he took me to the chapel. "I've got you a Cambridge gown and MA hood," he informed me. When I protested, he replied: "Yes, you must, all our preachers wear their appropriate gowns. And you must process in behind the choir – and speak from the pulpit, or you won't be heard." It was too late to protest further.

In front of me were rows of small boys, some way behind them were older boys, and somewhere behind them were staff and parents. I'd have to shout to reach my target audience. I've no idea what I said. Hopefully neither do they. At lunch with the headmaster and prefects, nobody could think of anything to say. I never got a thank you letter.

A friend of mine suffered similarly. He was invited to give a grand lecture at St Bride's church in Fleet Street – on the inevitable, but specious, topic of press ethics. Meeting him on the way in, I remarked on the importance of the lecture – it was to be printed and published. "What?", he said, "I thought I was just meeting a discussion group."

He was introduced by the editor of the *Times*. After ten minutes or so, he had said all he had to say. The editor of the *Times* gave a thank you speech which filled the full hour.

More travail
Lloyd's and my not-that-adventurous holidays took us to a surprising number of war zones.

We booked a cruise up the Nile from Aswan to Cairo in one of the wooden vessels beloved of Agatha Christie. (For the record, it was superb.) Before flying to Aswan, we booked a few nights at the Mena House Hotel near the Pyramids and ended up staying rather longer than expected. The Egyptian riot police had decided to riot themselves and chosen Mena House as their rallying point. We were confined to barracks until the crisis passed, hearing general hubbub and rifle fire as we followed instructions and cowered inside.

As we were eventually leaving, sitting next to us on the coach was an American tourist clutching a large lampshade, which he turned around to reveal a large bullet hole in the silk. Against all instructions he had gone out onto the balcony of his room to see what was happening. A security policeman took a pot shot, which missed. The hotel had suggested he keep the lampshade as a souvenir.

Another time, in Morocco in 1975, we were enjoying a few days on the beach at Agadir before heading to Marrakesh (Churchill's favourite hotel and all that), while Moroccan tanks rumbled past on their way to subdue rebels in Western Sahara.

The year before, we were in Athens having fled Mykonos when the Turks were invading Greek territory, principally Cyprus (later, we stayed at the island beach hotel from which British citizens had been evacuated by a destroyer). Lloyd and I had gone our own ways during the day and agreed to meet for a drink in Syntagma (Constitution) Square before dinner, where in those days you could still have a peaceful ouzo. I arrived first and found a shop selling English newspapers – the *Financial Times*, to be precise. I was sitting reading the pink paper when Lloyd arrived. "What are you doing? Don't you know that the students are demonstrating just across the road?"

My mother and father didn't know much about any of this. Except the Mena House riot. This made the British newspapers and my mother got herself into a state of high indignation, largely at me for not calling her to say we were still alive. The British ambassador was ordered out of bed to find out where we were.

And finally…

At the Publishers Association, our relationships with authors' bodies weren't always as happy as we both wanted. When I arrived, the PA was under attack for not supporting authors in their fight to be remunerated when their books were loaned out by public libraries – now established, by law, as the Public Lending Right. Fresh from Fleet Street, I decided the first step was to get to know your adversaries, so I invited the more ardent authors' leaders, the novelists Brigid Brophy and Maureen Duffy, and Elaine Steele, director of the Writers' Guild, to lunch at the Grange, a leading Covent Garden restaurant. I arrived with two colleagues to find them already well installed. We did our best to catch up until the head waiter appeared with the menu. Ms Brophy gave me what I can only describe as a hostile glare. "You don't seem to realise, Mr Bradley, that we are all vegetarians."

"Oh, but I do, Ms Brophy, which is why I chose this restaurant", I responded, pointing to the immaculate display of fresh Covent Garden specialities. "Huh" said Brigid, "We are not … RABBITS!"

INDEX

death 151
and EEC 108
Feliks Topolski's portrait of 72
and General Election (1970) 30
and Gerald Kaufman 63
and Hugh Cudlipp 89–90
and Joe Haines 201
and Lord Chalfont (Alun Gwynne-Jones) 49
and Lord Goodman 147, 150, 151
MI5 and 64, 195
and public inquiries into press 97
retirement 85–86, 149, 158
and Royal Commission on the Press 143
succeeds Hugh Gaitskell 50, 54, 57, 61
and Tony Benn 59
Wilson, Mary 62, 79
Winchester Arts Festival 46
Windjammer (film) 24
Windsor Castle, Berkshire 109
  Royal Library 109, 145
Women in Publishing 163
Women's Institutes 184
Woollings, Mr 37
World Bank 167
World Trade Organisation 179
World Wide Web 210
Worlock, David 209–10
Wright, Peter 64

Spycatcher 64, 195
Writers' Guild 183, 235
Wurmser charts 71
Wyatt, Woodrow 82
Wycherley, William, *The Country Wife* 21
Wycliffe College, Gloucestershire 232–33

Yale Law School Journal 23
Yale University, New Haven, Connecticut 16, 20, 25, 27–29, 37, 44
  Beinecke Rare Book and Manuscript Library 23
  Berkeley College 20–23
    Master's Lodge 21
  Commonplace Society 21
  Cross-Campus 20
  Elizabethan Club 23, 28
  Graduate Club 22
  Graduate School 25
  Law School 21–24
  Mellon Fellowship 18
  Sterling Library 20, 28
  Yale Center for British Art 23, 25, 28
Yamani, Ahmed Zaki, Sheikh 85
Yeltsin, Boris 192
Yemen 75, 86
Yes Minister 80

Zambia 48
Zimbabwe 48

Milton Keynes UK
Ingram Content Group UK Ltd.
UKHW020018120724
445119UK00005B/52/J

9 781738 497058